THE HISTORY OF NORWAY

FROM THE ICE AGE TO TODAY

ØIVIND STENERSEN
IVAR LIBÆK

© This translation, James Anderson 2003

DINAMO FORLAG

© 2003 Dinamo Forlag

Graphic design and jacket: Mona Dahl
Picture editor: Tone Svinningen
Maps: Geir Tandberg Steigan
This book is set in FFScala 9,5/12,2
Paper: 115 g Arctic Volume
Repro: Iris Digital
Impression: Stalling
Binding: Stalling
First edition

ISBN 82-8071-041-8

All correspondence concerning
this book may be sent to
Dinamo Forlag
Postboks 442, 1327 Lysaker, Norway
Tlf: 67 200 000

www.dinamo.no

Contents

From the Ice Age to the Iron Age

Up to 800 A.D.

Hunting and sealing cultures in Palaeolithic times (prior to 4000 B.C.)

About 14,000 years ago parts of the Norwegian coastline emerged from the ice masses that had covered northern Europe for several thousand years. The Norwegian Channel separated the south-west corner of the country from the Continent in the south, but in cold winters that area of sea must have been covered with ice. The climate was arctic and the landscape was characterised by tundra vegetation including heather, willow scrub and dwarf birch.

We shall never know if the first people to cross the Norwegian Channel used boats or migrated across one cold winter's day, but there is much to suggest that they were tempted northwards by bounteous food resources. At that time the Norwegian coast with its innumerable holms and skerries must have held a much greater promise of hunting, sealing and fishing than the endless shallows along the North Sea mainland. We must also remember, when considering that first immigration, that the plains of northern Germany were being covered in forest. Flocks of wild reindeer would therefore have moved northwards towards the Scandinavian glaciers, and a number of reindeer hunters would have followed them.

Wild reindeer have lived high in the Norwegian mountains ever since the last Ice Age. Today the largest flock of wild reindeer can be found on the Hardanger Plateau.

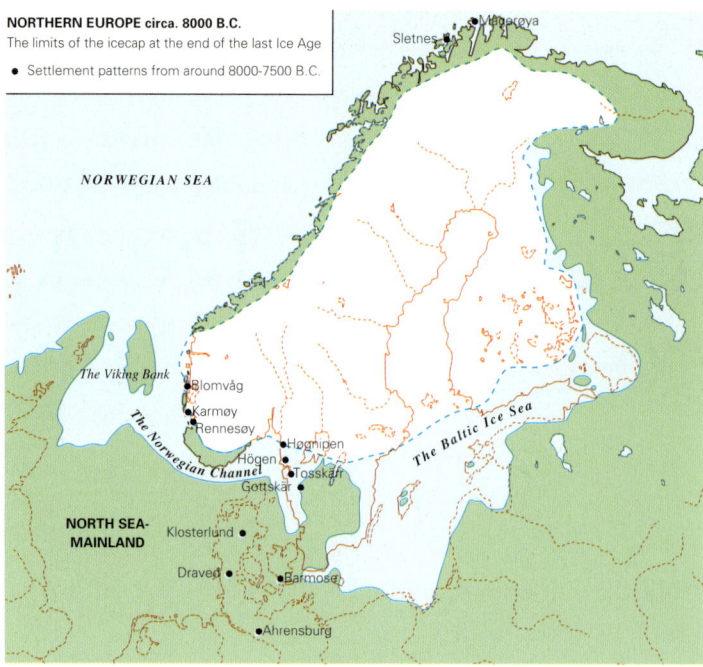

NORWEGIAN SEA

Magerøya
Sletnes

The Viking Bank
●Blomvåg
●Karmøy
●Rennesøy
The Norwegian Channel
●Høgnipen
Høgen●
●Tosskär
Gottskär

The Baltic Ice Sea

NORTH SEA-
MAINLAND
Klosterlund ●
Draved ● ●Barmose
●Ahrensburg

The first hunters lived in small groups that moved about a lot. Presumably they had light tents and skin-covered boats that allowed them to move across large areas. As early as 9300 B.C. some of them had got as far as Magerøya near Nordkapp in Finnmark.

From about 8000 B.C. the ice began to recede rapidly, and from then on settlement spread along the entire coastline. The oldest Stone Age finds in north Troms and Finnmark are known as Komsa culture, from a settlement in Komsafjellet near Alta. In the rest of the country, finds from the period around 7000 B.C. are called Fosna culture after an excavation site at Fosna near Kristiansund. Both cultures had weapons and tools of the same kind, but they used different stone materials: flint dominated in the south, whereas the Komsa hunters used quartz and quartzite.

In southern Norway the Fosna culture was supplanted by the Nøstvet culture from about 7000 B.C. This new culture got its name from a site on the farm of Nøstvet at Ås south of Oslo. Characteristic of the Nøstvet hunters are their elongated, oval axes with a honed edge, made from volcanic rocks. Large parts of the country now began to enjoy a climate that compares with that of

southern England today. Temperate tree species like elm, lime, ash and oak began to take hold in the south of the country at lower altitudes, while pine and birch forest gave a new look to the mountain regions and northern Norway. Deer, wild boar, bears and elk made their way up from the south. Tree-felling and hunting in the great forests now demanded tougher axes and new weapons.

The Nøstvet hunters preferred settling in sheltered bays along the coast where they fished, caught seals and hunted in the forests. Some also trekked into the mountains reindeer hunting and trout fishing. The men were probably mainly responsible for the hunting, while the women and children stayed near the settlements. They gathered firewood, edible roots, berries, mussels and birds' eggs.

Around 4000 B.C. the people in north Troms and Finnmark began to use slate tools and earthenware, innovations that indicate they had close contact with the Stone Age cultures of Finland and Russia. The similarity between rock carvings at Alta and in northwest Russia points in a similar direction. The use of skis, sleds and large boats made of skin enabled the people of the north to travel hundreds of kilometres in just a few months.

Northern Europe's largest collection of Stone Age rock art was discovered at Alta in Finnmark. In 1985 these rock carvings were placed on UNESCO's list of international cultural monuments worthy of the highest protection.

In the last millennium before the birth of Christ, Finno-Ugric immigrants arrived in northern Scandinavia from the east. They appear to have assimilated with the original population of hunters, and together they developed the Sami (Lapp) language and culture.

Rock carvings from the Bronze Age at Skjeberg in Østfold. Rock paintings of this period appear to have one main purpose: to promote fertility in the fields and in animals and human beings.

The Neolithic period. The advent of farming. (4000–1800 B.C.)

Pollen analyses from bogs show that the first farming arrived in the areas around Oslofjord about 4000 B.C., roughly 5000 years after it had first been developed in the Middle East. Finds of slender-necked, honed axes and a special type of clay pot, known as Funnel-Beaker earthenware, indicate that knowledge of farming came from southern Scandinavia.

The first farmers scorched off the forest, sowed corn in the ashes and harvested it until the soil was completely exhausted. Then they moved on to new settlements. Initially, animal farming was probably of more importance than crop growing, and for a long while, hunting, sealing and fishing continued to be more important than farming in the interior and far north.

The great agricultural breakthrough came during the four centuries prior to 2500 B.C. During this period people began to grow oats or barley and keep pigs, cattle, sheep and goats right up the coast as far as Alta, and the same pattern was repeated in the valleys of the south. This development is often coupled with the arrival of the *Battle-Axe people* in Norway. This group takes its name from the beautiful honed stone axes found in their graves. The *Battle-Axe people* brought with them a culture which not only included new burial rites, weapons and tools, but which also may have carried the Indo-European language northwards. Norwegian developed from Indo-European, as did the majority of other European languages.

The Bronze Age (1800–500 B.C.)

This period saw important changes in agriculture. It became common to plough fields with a primitive wooden plough called an *ard*, horses came in use for riding and ploughing and new flint sickles made harvesting easier. Farmers now became more settled and began to build farms with permanent houses and yards. They favoured areas of dry moraine soil, as found on the ridges around Oslofjord, by Lake Mjøsa, in Jæren and in Trøndelag.

These bone fish-hooks from Kjelmøy in Finnmark, dating from the centuries immediately prior to the birth of Christ, come from the oldest Sami culture in Scandinavia.

Harvests got so large that some farmers had a surplus which enabled them to procure luxury goods from far away. They probably bartered for such goods with products that were in demand in other parts of Europe, especially furs and skins. The gorgeous finds from graves of the period are a clear indication of new riches: elegant flint daggers, amber jewellery, tools, weapons and ornamental articles made of bronze and costly gold trinkets. Many of these status symbols were imported from Jutland, which was a centre of Scandinavian Bronze Age culture. The metals of which bronze was composed were not mined in Scandinavia. The tin came from England and the copper from Hungary, but many moulds were made from the soapstone found in the mountainous areas of southern Norway.

Such luxuries, however, were of little importance to the majority of people. They continued to use stone, bone and wood for making tools, and for them it was probably more important that their womenfolk learnt to spin and weave so that the pelts they wore could be replaced with clothes made of sheep's wool.

The impressive Bronze Age burial mounds are visible evidence that society became more tiered and that the chieftains of the time had a high status. These monuments are often sited on elevated ground or as landmarks on headlands along the coast.

The Iron Age (500 B.C.–800 A.D.)

In the centuries immediately prior to the birth of Christ the temperature fell and precipitation increased, until weather conditions were roughly similar to the ones we have now. In western Norway and the northern half of the country the temperate deciduous forest was replaced with pine and birch. In eastern parts, forests of spruce began to take over.

The shift in climate meant that farmers had to erect more buildings to give shelter to both people and animals. These new structures were usually built in locations with dry sandy soil. It is in such places we find the oldest farm names in the country, and these names often describe the natural features of the place, for example Ås (ridge), Haug (knoll), Åker (field) or Sander (sands).

In southern Scandinavia the first period of the Iron Age, from 500 B.C. until the birth of Christ is known as the *Celtic Iron Age*. The name indicates that it was the Celts who introduced a know-

A Roman glass chalice from Klepp in Jæren, Rogaland.

A clothes clasp from the farm of Åker at Vang in Hedmark. This piece has been dated to the end of the 6th century A.D. and has a motif that may show Frankish influences.

ledge of iron into this part of Europe. The new metal was made from ore that was easily accessible in bogs, and most people were now able to equip themselves with knives, sickles, axes, arrow heads and other weapons and tools made from iron. These iron implements made it easier to cultivate the land. Harvests got larger and the population grew. As a result, land for more farms was cleared.

In the earliest Iron Age farms several generations dwelt under the same roof. When the sons got married, they remained on the farm with their wives and children. This type of extended family was called a clan. It had to defer to the clan patriarchs and matriarchs who were the heads of the farm. They ensured that ancient traditions were upheld, and were living links to the clan's dead leaders who were worshipped as gods. The clan gave security and protection to everyone who belonged to it. Everyone could expect help from their clan when they became sick, old or came in conflict with other clans.

If differences arose between the clans in an area due to murder, theft or badly defined farm boundaries, all freemen would assemble at the *Ting*. This was a sacred place where force of any sort was forbidden. Many cases decided by the *ting* would end in one party having to compensate another. Such a fine was usually paid in corn, butter or cattle. In serious cases the offender might be outlawed. This meant that any freeman was entitled to kill him.

During the first four centuries after the birth of Christ the Roman Empire was the economic and political powerhouse of Europe, and the Scandinavian peoples took many impulses from it. Thus the period is also called the *Roman Iron Age*, except in the Sami areas. The Scandinavian peoples developed their own letters, runes, from the Latin alphabet, and adopted the Roman system of weights.

During the Roman Iron Age a lively trade existed between north and south. From trading posts at the mouth of the Rhine and along the Baltic, various Roman luxury goods were transported to Zealand and further northwards. The graves of important contemporary farmers have yielded Roman bronze vessels, gold and silver jewellery, glassware and swords. These goods would presumably have been traded for furs, down, animal skins and slaves. It is possible, too, that some Scandinavian dignitaries brought luxury goods home with them after serving as Roman mercenaries.

Finds from graves constructed in the post-Christian era clearly show that the ruling or chieftain's clans, *høvdingættene*, on the largest farms became richer and more influential in a number areas. Gradually, as the population of communities grew, so did the need for common rules, and iron production was sufficiently labour intensive and complex to need organisation by a supervisory authority.

The chieftains also functioned as priests during the feasts for gods like Njord and Frøya. During these sacrifices (*blot*) the farmers would hand over produce from their farms to the chieftain. A part of these sacrificial gifts were used by the chieftain to pay professional soldiers. A band of such warriors was called a *hird*. This enabled the chieftain to increase his power over the people within his own kingdom and subjugate other tribes. A tribe consisted of people from several settlements within a kingdom or land. Today we see traces of these chieftains' domains in geographical names such as Rogaland and Ringerike (*rike* = realm).

During the troubled period of *Germanic tribal migrations* from 400 to 550 A.D. farmers seemed to want to imbue the chieftains with greater powers to organise and lead the defence of the districts. An important element in this work was the building of simple fortifications, hill forts, where people and animals could seek shelter in times of trouble. These local defences may have been set up to defend against foreign tribes who arrived in the country after the fall of the Western Roman Empire. Two place names in western Norway hint at such immigration. Rogaland can be linked to the *rygene*, a tribe that lived on the Baltic coast and gave its name to the Rügen Peninsula, while Hordaland can be traced to the *hordene*, a tribe whose name is reflected in the German district called Harz.

At the end of the 6th century A.D. parts of the country were thrown into crisis. In south-western Norway hundreds of farms were deserted and the population must have fallen significantly. A possible explanation of this population loss is plague, which is described in contemporary annals from both Gaul and the British Isles. It is probable that these epidemics also spread to Scandinavia.

But in the 7th century a new period of prosperity began. Deserted farms were brought back into use, ground for new farms and summer farms was cleared, and fishing hamlets grew up along the coast. The production of iron and soapstone products increased once more, and trade around the North Sea blossomed.

The upturn was related to developments in the Frankish kingdom where the Merovingian dynasty had founded a new and stable kingdom. The Merovingian kings were models for the chieftain clans of northern Europe and it is with good reason the final pre-historic period, from 550 to 800 A.D., is called the *Merovingian Period* in Norway. Finds of ornaments, helmets and ringed swords bear witness to close links with the Franks. These Frankish luxury goods came from opulent trading centres along the North Sea coast, the most important of which was Dorestad in Friesland.

During the 8th century it is apparent that certain chieftain clans increased their power and prestige at the expense of others. One important cause of this development was that some clans gained greater interest in, and control of, foreign trade. The most powerful clans appear to have lived near Borre in Vestfold, at Åker by Lake Mjøsa, in Ytre Namdalen in Trøndelag, on Karmsundet in Rogaland and at Borg on Vestvågøy in Nordland. Here lay much of the foundation for the economic expansion and political unification of the country that was to gather pace in the coming centuries.

The Viking Age
800–1030

Expansion from Scandinavia

In the year 793 some Norse sea-raiders attacked the monastery of Lindisfarne on the north-east coast of England. This event is generally considered to be the beginning of the Viking age. From the end of the 8th century and up to the middle of the 11th, Scandinavian peoples played a leading role in European history for the first time. During this period Swedes, Danes and Norwegians set out on sea voyages to distant lands and coasts. Their expeditions reached the steppes of Russia in the east, the Mediterranean, the Black Sea and the Caspian Sea in the south, the Barents Sea in the north and America in the west.

The word viking may be a derivation of the Old Norse name for Oslofjord, *Viken*, but in the Europe of the time Vikings were given other nicknames. In Byzantium they were called *væringer*. The Slavs in the east usually called them *rus*, the English spoke of them as *Danes*, while with the Franks they went under the name *northmen*.

Vikings are no longer merely regarded as raiders and murderers. Nowadays we emphasise the fact that the Vikings were also skilled ship builders, craftsmen, seafarers, explorers and merchants. They colonised large areas, founded towns and founded new kingdoms.

Recent archaeological excavations and examination of written sources from Western Europe, Arabia and Byzantium provide us with a more subtle picture. Frankish and Anglo-Saxon chronicles, Arabian travelogues, runic inscriptions and Icelandic sagas form the main strands in a rich written record. It is large enough to consider regarding the Viking age as the beginning of historical time in Scandinavia.

Odin, the god of war, was one-eyed because, according to Norse mythology, he had given his right eye to Mime, owner of the Well of Wisdom, which lay under the tree of the world, Yggdrasil. Wood sculpture from Gamlebyen, the oldest part of Oslo.

Background to the Viking journeys

The longship is the very symbol of the Viking age. It represents the acme of the Vikings' technical feats. The ship had a solid keel, an elastic hull and efficient sails, enabling the Vikings to make long open sea journeys under all conditions. Despite being low amidships, the boats could weather high seas. Their draft was very small, too, and they could be rowed up shallow rivers. On board were kitchen utensils, tents and non-perishable food that enabled the Vikings to undertake long journeys in inhospitable and uninhabited regions. The ships could be hauled up on sand beaches and, if necessary, rolled along on logs between rivers and past rapids. Ships with such attributes gave the Vikings great scope of action. They could move rapidly, attack unexpectedly and withdraw quickly.

The Vikings were extremely good navigators. They set their course using the stars and by measuring the height of the sun. Descriptions of sea routes were handed down orally from father to son, and it was a matter of prestige to have knowledge of the currents, sea depths and wind conditions of other countries' coasts.

During the course of the Iron Age the population of Scandinavia rose as iron implements came into general use. People cleared new farms, and towards the end of the 8th century agricultural land in the west of Norway was in short supply. This must have been the main reason why people from that area crossed the sea to settle on the thinly populated islands of Shetland, Orkney, the Faroes and Hebridies.

Many Vikings set out on long journeys to enrich themselves by trade, and they developed a special vessel, the *knarren*, that was especially well adapted to mercantile transport. New trade routes through Scandinavia grew up during the Viking age, linking Western Europe to the Byzantine Empire and the caliphate of Baghdad. Swedish Vikings set up bases along the Russian rivers and forced the local inhabitants to pay them taxes in the form of slaves and furs. They sold these commodities on to the Arabs for silver coins, silk and other luxury items.

The trading centre of Birka near Mälaren in Sweden was an important junction for trade eastwards. Birka had close ties with Hedeby in Denmark which was Scandinavia's economic hub during the Viking age. From Hedeby trade routes radiated out to the Frankish kingdom, to the British Isles and northwards to Skiringssal in Vestfold.

Skiringssal was the largest trading centre in Norway in the 9th century. Archaeological remains provide us with interesting glimpses of the activity of the place. Amongst the imports have been found Arabian coins, Frankish glass and ornaments from Ireland. There are also traces left by craftsmen. Smiths, pearl-makers and goldsmiths had their own workshops. Pots, spinning wheels and soapstone moulds were important export products. So too, presumably, were tools and bars of iron, whetstones and goods from northern Norway such as whalebone, down, feathers, antlers, furs and walrus teeth. Furthermore, we can assume that amber, honey, precious metals, corn, salt, weapons, glass, wine and thralls were brought in. Thralls were slaves, and many of them had been taken prisoner in the manner described by the priest on Lindisfarne after the attack in 793.

Thralls were made to carry out much of the manual work on the largest farms. Digging, felling and grinding corn was typical thrall's

The Oseberg ship was excavated on the farm of Oseberg in Vestfold in 1904. The ship is 22 metres long and had room for 34 men at the oars. It was used as a burial chamber for a lady of high birth, and contained her slave woman and a rich assortment of equipment from the large farm she lived on.

work, and the need for the thralls increased when the menfolk were away at sea. Then the running of the farm was taken over by the women with the lady of the house in charge.

At the start of the Viking period it appears that Scandinavians sailed to foreign lands purely on trading missions. These journeys showed them that conditions were rife for plunder. In the first place, they must have realised that their ships were superior, and that coastal defences were poor. They also saw that it was easy to loot items of silver and gold from churches and monasteries. Back at home once more, such news spread fast and tempted others to follow suit.

It was not just their ships that made the Vikings a military threat. From a very early age small boys were taught to use weapons and to ride, and the weapons they used were efficient. The chief armament of the Vikings was the sword, preferably of the Frankish type and forged so that it did not break in battle. In addition, they had sharp axes with long shafts, bows and arrows and spears they could throw or lunge with. Chieftains and *hirdmenn* had coats of chain mail made of thousands small iron rings, while ordinary soldiers wore thick leather jerkins. As a protection against enemy weapons they wore conical helmets with nose protection and light wooden shields that had iron shield bosses protecting the handles.

The Vikings had an effective fighting organisation that was both feared and admired. They came together in warrior bands led by chieftains. The values of these professional warriors placed disregard of death, strength, weapons skills, heroic courage and personal sacrifice in highest regard. They worshipped the warrior god Odin, who they believed had the power of deciding victory and defeat on the battlefield. For a Viking it was better to be killed honourably in battle for his chieftain than to die of old age in his bed.

The Vikings believed that if they died in battle, Odin would take them to the heavenly realm of Valhalla, where they could fight all day and then be served meat and mead by beautiful women in the evening. This optimistic view of death may have given the Vikings a psychological advantage over Christians in warfare. Churches preached that, at worst, eternal torture with Satan in hell might be one's due after death.

A helmet from Gjermundbu in Buskerud. Viking helmets did not sport bull's horns.

Opposite page:
The Viking sword on the left is from Lødingen in Nordland. The other one was found at Åsnes in Hedmark

The Norwegian Viking expansion

Norwegians preferred journeying westwards, to the islands of the Atlantic, but they also took part in raids on the Russian rivers and in

Western Europe together with Swedes and Danes. The Vikings often fought each other, and they were quite capable of joining forces with Christian princes in order to fight other Vikings. On several occasions, chieftains from various parts of Scandinavia also came together in large armies to storm wealthy cities or large tracts of land.

Early in the 9th century the Vikings' practice was to launch small attacks along coasts and up rivers. Such forays continued to play an important part in Viking tactics, but from the middle of the 9th century they began to overwinter on islands that were situated conveniently for further operations. In 843, for example, Vikings from Vestfold attacked Nantes in the Frankish kingdom. They plundered and burnt the town before building a base on the island of Noirmoutier in the mouth of the River Loire. From there they launched plundering raids inland forcing the inhabitants to pay them tax on the wine and salt trade. Later on, the Norwegian Vikings joined forces with the Danes and set out on expeditions to Spain and on into the Mediterranean.

The chief destination for the Norwegian Vikings was the British Isles; from the newly settled colonies of Shetland, the Faroes, Orkneys and Hebridies they pushed southwards and settled in northern Scotland, on Man and on the eastern side of the Irish Sea. Right up until the 18th century the inhabitants of Shetland and Orkney spoke Old Norwegian, and a myriad of place names still bear witness to the Norwegian settlement.

The Danes, who had conquered most of England, competed with the Norwegians for the control of York. The city was one of the largest trading centres north of the Alps in the Viking age.

When the Norwegians arrived in Ireland shortly after 800, they had an easy time of it; the island was split into small kingdoms that were constantly at war with one another. The Vikings settled along the coast, founded the first towns, introduced coins and began trading with the rest of Europe. However, their brutal behaviour led the Celtic inhabitants to unite against them. The Irish had been especially provoked by the chieftain Turgeis, who founded Dublin. Wanting to replace Christianity with the worship of Thor the thunder god, Turgeis built a heathen temple at Armagh, which was the main seat of the Christian church on the island. The Celts took the chieftain prisoner and drowned him.

The Celts soon learnt from the Vikings how to build better ships and weapons. The Irish petty kings allied themselves with the Danes

and, around the year 900, the Norwegians were driven out. But they returned. It was only at the beginning of the 11th century that the final Norwegian Viking kingdom in Ireland was vanquished.

A party of Vikings who had been blown off course on their way from Norway to the British Isles, discovered Iceland in the second half of the 9th century. The country was already inhabited by Irish monks at the time, but they left the island as soon as the Vikings began to settle there. The majority of the settlers were from western Norway, and some of them had left Norway because they refused to pay allegiance to King Harald Fairhair who was trying to unify the country into one kingdom. Many also came from the Norwegian districts of Scotland and Ireland.

By about 930 the whole of Iceland had been divided up between just over four hundred chieftains. They instituted their own legislature, the *Allting*, taking its laws from the western Norwegian legal assembly, the *Gulating*. However, the vast bulk of the inhabitants were thralls of Irish and Scottish descent, who had rapidly to relinquish their Celtic culture.

Iceland became a seat of Norse saga literature. The sagas are one

The "baroque" animal-head post from the Oseberg find. Presumably the post served a religious function.

of the main sources of our knowledge about the Vikings and medieval society. Although they were written down several centuries after the events they describe, they contain a wealth of reliable information. The "Sagas of the Norwegian Kings" are based on a number of lays written by the skalds of the Viking kings. The lays were rhymed, and were preserved word for word for generations until they were written down by Snorre Sturlason and the other saga writers.

The sagas relate that the first Vikings settled in Greenland in the 980s. The colonisation was led by Eirik the Red from Rogaland, who had been outlawed after a murder in Iceland. From there he took twenty-five ships fully laden with people, animals and equipment to the new land. Only fourteen ships survived the journey. In the ensuing years more than 250 farms were set up in Austbygda and almost eighty in Vestbygda. These communities lasted until around the year 1500 when the population died out for reasons unknown.

Around the year 1000, Eirik's son Leiv led an expedition along the coast of North America. He overwintered on the tip of Newfoundland at a place which is now called L'Anse aux Meadows. The area was named Vinland, which presumably means "land of the fine grass plains". Several others journeyed to Vinland, but no permanent settlement was established there. Attacks from Indians may have been one reason for this.

The unification of Norway

In the 9th century the population from Oslofjord to southern Troms spoke one language, a language distinct from that of neighbouring peoples, and even though settlements were cut off from one another by mountains, forests, open country and fjords, there was a network of trading and clan ties that linked the regions together. But the country was still split up into small kingdoms ruled by powerful chieftains. They owned the biggest farms, were patriarchs of the richest clans, played the key role in the *ting* and were military and religious leaders.

In the second half of the 9th century a power struggle began between the chieftains. One of the combatants was fired with the ambition of gaining control of the whole of Norway. His name was Harald Fairhair and, according to Snorre, he belonged to Yngling clan from Vestfold who occupied a leading position in eastern Norway. Several historians have linked Harald Fairhair's clan to the rich memorials from Oseberg and Gokstad. Harald may have derived income from trade at Skiringssal and wanted to secure the sea route northwards up the Norwegian coast. The problem was that Vikings from western Norway were continually attacking ships on their way from Trøndelag and northern Norway to Skiringssal. Probably to put an end to this piracy, Harald travelled to Trøndelag. There he made a pact with the powerful family of the Lade earls who had big trading interests in the north. Together they began a campaign against the petty kings of western Norway. At the end of the 9th century Harald won a decisive battle at Hafrsfjord in Rogaland.

Harald did not set up a large state administration. Together with his warriors, the hird, he travelled round his kingdom on a progress, a *veitsle*: when the King arrived in a country district, the farmers had to provide overnight accommodation, food and beer. Harald also lived on his royal estates, several of which had belonged to chieftains who had fallen or fled during the battles of unification. The King instituted stewards, *årmenn*, as factors and policemen on his estates. They were charged with maintaining peace and order in the districts; they punished wrong-doers and collected fines from those who had broken the laws. Here we see the King beginning to usurp the clans' ancient right to punish offences.

Harald was also concerned to secure his kingdom from foreign threat. He attacked Vikings on the Atlantic islands and sent one of his sons, Håkon, to be fostered with King Athelstan in England, where he was converted to Christianity.

Harald had several sons, and when he died in about 930, a bloody feud arose over the realm. Håkon was victorious and was adopted as king by the *Øreting* in Trøndelag. There he pledged to respect and improve the laws. Håkon was nicknamed "the Good", partly because he kept his promise and partly, also, because he gave up his attempts to introduce Christianity.

In conjunction with the farmers of western Norway and Trøndelag, Håkon established a new *ting* system. At the two new common or *lagtings*, the *Gulating* and the *Frostating*, delegates from each of the two regions met. The stewards selected the representatives, and the King came to the *ting* to discuss relevant matters. The common *ting* handed down judgements and framed laws under the guidance of a special legal expert, a law speaker (*lagmannen*). He recited the laws and interpreted them before the *ting* took its final decision.

Håkon got the common *tings* to inaugurate a system of defence which was called *leidang*. The law now required farmers to furnish longships with crew and equipment for two months' service. The ships were to be under the King's command and would be summoned with the help of beacons.

The *lagting* and *leidang* systems strengthened the national monarchy and the Fairhair dynasty, but there were still people who would not accept that *one* family of chieftains could be allowed to dominate the others. After the death of Håkon the Good in 960, the Lade earls in Trøndelag went into league with Danish kings who wanted control of the area around Oslofjord. Right up until the 1030s they stood united against the Fairhair dynasty's attempts to gain royal power in Norway.

Norwegian unification is part of a larger picture. In several parts of Europe kings and princes were creating new states, and Scandinavians who came into contact with these could not avoid bringing ideas of a strengthened monarchy back home with them. Sweden and Denmark were unified into distinct realms at the same time as Norway.

Fairhair kinsmen Olav Tryggvason and Olav Haraldsson tried to take up the inheritance from Håkon the Good. They were both great fighters who had amassed huge wealth on Viking expeditions, especially in England. They used it to pay for armed retainers and buy support from Norwegian chieftains. However, they had powerful enemies. In 1000, after only five years' struggle, Olav Tryggvason fell at the battle of Svolder.

On their sallies into Europe the two Olavs had become Christians and on their return, they attempted to introduce Christianity by force. Although by the end of the 10th century the new doctrine had gained a foothold along the coast, many were opposed to it, particularly in inland areas in the east and north.

It must have been hard for chieftains and ordinary farmers to reject their ancient religion which had permeated both working day

A gravestone from Lindisfarne which shows Vikings attacking in about 800 A.D. On the back, two monks are depicted praying at a cross.

and feast for centuries. To placate their gods the people had made sacrifices and carried out various rituals. These sacred acts were carried out in special groves, in the fields, on burial mounds or stone altars and in houses containing idols (*hov*). Large feasts, *blot*, were held several times a year in honour of the gods. During such feasts, leading men and women from the chieftain clan, called *goder* and *gydjer,* would act as sacrificial priests.

It was these customs Olav Haraldsson wanted to end when he arrived in the country in 1015 to make himself king. His timing was propitious. The Danish king, Olav's most powerful adversary, was busy with a big campaign in England, making it easier for Olav to beat the Lade earls and build up a new kingdom.

Olav got several *tings* to pass a special church law that paved the way for the new religion. The new measures had the effect of transferring religious authority from the family and home to the church. The King tore down *hovs* and smashed idols, building churches in their place and instituting a priesthood with himself at its head. Those who refused to yield frequently had to pay with their lives or watch their farms go up in flames.

Many chieftains feared that Christianity would rob them of their position as religious leaders and heads of clans, their priestly role being closely linked to the influence they had at the *ting* and as military leaders. It is therefore hardly surprising that Olav made many enemies in areas where the old religion was strongest.

It was essential for Olav to win over the country's most powerful clans. He offered them income from his own estates and let them take over some of his stewards' functions. By way of return they had to swear allegiance to him. A chieftain who bound himself to the King in this way was called a *lendmann.*

The majority of powerful men were not content with the prestige that the position of *lendmann* would give them. Although several were Christians, they feared that Olav would have too much control over them. It was therefore not difficult for the Danish King, Knut the Great, to garner support from the Norwegian chieftains when, in 1025, he decided to incorporate Norway into his North Sea kingdom.

Olav had to flee the country, but he returned to take up the struggle. In 1030 he faced his enemies at Stiklestad in Trøndelag. The battle ended with the King being cut down and killed. It all now looked very much as if the Fairhair dynasty had lost the battle for the crown of Norway.

The gold hoard from Hoen at Øvre Eiker in Buskerud is the biggest found in Norway. It included a number of coins of Arabian, Byzantine and Frankish origin.

The Middle Ages

1030–1537

King and church 1030–1130

After Olav's fall, Knut the Great's illegitimate son, Svein Alfivason, became King of Norway. The boy was ten years old, and his mother went with him to help him rule. But Danish power felt like a yoke. New taxes weighed farmers down, and poor yields meant food shortages. Svein got a bad reputation because he was not attended by luck and good fortune.

But Svein's rule was also challenged by Olav himself. After the battle of Stiklestad some farmers had secretly taken the King's corpse away. They buried it in sand by the River Nid, and soon rumours of miracles began to circulate. The bishop of Olav's *hird* travelled northwards to Nidaros and, one year after his death, the King's body was exhumed in the presence of the leading figures in the land. Legend has it that Olav was as well preserved as the day he had been buried, and that his beard and hair had grown. The body was placed in a casket in St Clement's Church, and the *hird* bishop elevated Olav to the sainthood. Norway's kings had now been linked to God in perpetuity, and Olav's descendants would have a special claim to the Norwegian throne. Olav had become *rex perpetuus Norvegiae* – "the Eternal King of Norway", and the country had got its patron saint.

In the centuries that followed, groups of pilgrims made their way to Nidaros. They came from every part of Norway, from the rest of Scandinavia, from England and the Continent. Like Rome in the south, Jerusalem in the east and Santiago de Compostela in the west, Nidaros in the north became one of the main destinations for

Altarpiece depicting the life and death of Saint Olav, probably originating from the stave church in Haltdalen in Trøndelag around 1300. After the Reformation in 1537 the altarpiece was sent to Denmark, but it was returned during the jubilee celebrations for the Saint Olav millenium in 1930. It is now housed in Nidaros Cathedral in Trondheim.

pilgrims in medieval times. The pilgrims and those who lived along the pilgrim routes swapped tales of the King's deeds, and in the 12th century the priests at Nidaros gathered these stories in a book they called *Passio Olavi* (Olav's Passion). Transcripts of this book have been found in Finland, England, France and Austria, and this says something about just how widespread the cult of St Olav became in the Middle Ages.

The saintly King became a symbol of unity, and his enemies acknowledged that he had shown his power after death. So unpopular had Danish rule become by 1034 that one of Olav's slayers at Stiklestad, one Kalv Arnesson, went to Gardarike where the King's eleven-year-old son, Magnus, was living. The following year Magnus came to Norway and assumed the title of king. Svein and his mother left the country without offering any resistance.

During the century between Olav's fall and the death of King Sigurd the Crusader there was peace at home. Norway entered a period of lavish growth and its first cities were founded. After 1030 a central monarchy was universally accepted. During the Viking age many great men had been despotic, and so the average farmer may well have felt that a national king and his men might be some protection. Danish rule also taught Norwegians that their country could be threatened from abroad, and although it would be an exaggeration to talk of national unity, the people of Trøndelag and Vestfold felt they had more in common with each other than with the Danes.

After Christianity arrived the old customs lived on, but in new guises. Yuletide festivities continued, but they were now celebrated in the names of Jesus and the Virgin Mary. Christianity took over the functions that the clan system and the heathen gods had occupied. Mass replaced sacrifice, and even though people understood very little of what went on in church, the mysterious ceremony had a unifying quality, with a sermon in Latin, beautiful pictures and strange fragrances. The individual became part of a new brotherhood – the Christian one.

Right from the start the King was the head of the Norwegian church. Only in 1152 did Norway become a separate ecclesiastical province with an archbishopric in Nidaros. The church needed the King's authority to enable Christianity to take root properly, whereas the King derived great benefit from the organisation of the church, and the church doctrine that the King derived his power from God was hardly a disadvantage. The people, too, slowly found

Borgund stave church at Lærdal, Sogn og Fjordane, the best preserved of the country's stave churches, was built in the second half of the 12th century. It is one of roughly 800 wooden churches built during the Middle Ages.

In 1066 the Norwegian king, Harald Hardrada, sailed to England and laid claim to the throne. But the king lost his life at the battle of Stamford Bridge near York. This detail is from the Bayeux Tapestry, woven to commemorate Duke William of Normandy who won the battle of Hastings and took the throne of England in that year.

their place in the new organisation. And so, during that century of peace, the Norwegian church became not merely a royal church, but also a church of the people.

By the middle of the 12th century both the King's power and the church's authority were uncontested in Norway. But if King and church triumphed with their orders and decrees, there had to be losers.

Peasant society

Between the years 1000 and 1300 the population of Norway increased from 150,000 to around 400,000 and new land was put under the plough. In the east of the country 5,000 farms were cleared, and the commonness of Norwegian names that end in -rud (clearing) bear witness to that. Population growth also necessitated the division of farms, particularly in the west where there was little arable land.

During the Viking period farmers owned their own land, but three hundred years later much of it had changed ownership. The majority of farmers had become tenants of the King, the church or the aristocracy, who together owned about 70% of the land. Huge forces had contributed to this change of ownership. When Norway had been unified, the kings confiscated the land of farmers who opposed them. The monarchy also laid claim to land that no one else owned, and this turned every farmer who cleared new ground into a tenant of the King. During the 12th and 13th centuries population pressure increased, and if the crops failed, a farmer might be forced to borrow from the King, the church or a nobleman to get his family through the winter. If he failed to repay what he owed, the lender would assume ownership of all, or part, of his farm. The farmer could continue working his farm, but now only as a tenant. At the same time it was common for kings and noblemen, and occasionally ordinary farmers too, to give land to the church so that priests would pray for their souls. Such gifts helped to make the church Norway's largest landowner.

But Norwegian farmers enjoyed greater freedoms than farmers who lived on large manors in other parts of Europe. The Norwegian landlords owned individual farms that were miles apart, or they might only own parts of a farm. The country was long and hard to travel, and the landlord's visits could be few and far between. The Norwegian farmer was legally free throughout the whole of the Middle Ages and he was not seen as socially degraded because he was a tenant; a tenant farmer on good land could be in a better position than one who owned his own farm.

The drudgery of the farmer and his family provided a living for his masters: The landlord wanted rents, the king taxes and the church tithes. Farmers had to maintain churches and supply transport for the King's men travelling through the district, and both King and church could impose fines if people broke the law. An average farmer of the 13th century had to relinquish about 20% of what his family produced to the King, the church and the aristocracy.

Civil war 1130–1217

In the 1120s an Irishman, Gilchrist (Christ's servant), came to Norway demanding to be made king. To prove that he was the son of Magnus Bareleg he walked over nine red-hot ploughshares, and according to the sagas his feet showed no signs of burns three days later. King Sigurd the Crusader, who was on the throne at this time, accepted this clear sign from God, but Gilchrist swore not to let himself be hailed as king before Sigurd and his son Magnus were dead. But the agreement was of little use: When Sigurd died in 1130, Magnus was hailed, but so, too, was Gilchrist who now called himself Harald Gille. Harald had Magnus mutilated and killed, but he himself was later killed by another pretender to the throne. Norway was in the throes of a period of civil war. However, this century of war should not be over dramatised. The population rose, more land was cultivated, the incomes of king and church increased and there were long periods of peace.

The royal right to succession was part of the reason for the civil war. Every king's son, whether legitimate or illegitimate, had the right to be a king, and they ruled together in shared sovereignty. Thanks to great good fortune, no internal divisions had surfaced in Norway during the hundred years of peace. After 1130 the pretenders were often small children backed by powerful chieftains with links to various regions of the country who were attempting to increase their own personal power, and this was another significant cause of the civil wars.

During the incursions of the civil war the church consolidated its position. Norway too felt the demand for church freedom – "libertas ecclesiae" – from temporal control. A movement, originating from the monastery of Cluny in Burgundy, maintained that temporal power was neither able to guard the church's interests nor foster peace in society. Therefore the church should shake itself free and run its own affairs.

When the archbishopric of Nidaros was established in 1152, the church attempted to create a monarchy it could mould and control. Accordingly, the archbishop supported the powerful Erling Skakke from the west of the country who was married to Kristin, daughter of King Sigurd the Crusader. He had a son, Magnus, by her. Magnus was not a king's son and so he had no right to be king, but because he was legitimate the church wanted him on the throne. Erling himself had won respect in ecclesiastical circles because in his youth he had taken part in a crusade in the Holy Land, and during a battle with the Arabs he had sustained a severe wound to his neck.

Erling Skakke saw the prospect of personal political gain, and he cut down other pretenders. In 1163 the archbishop crowned and anointed the seven-year-old Magnus Erlingsson as Norwegian King. At the same time a law was passed forbidding shared sovereignty; the King's eldest legitimate son was henceforth to have first claim on the throne.

However, Erling and Magnus found little peace. They were continually having to deal with pretenders, and in 1176 a man who had been

Nidaros Cathedral in Trondheim is the largest medieval building in Scandinavia, constructed in a West European style. The cathedral was erected over the remains of King Olav Kyrre's Christchurch of 1075, and the construction work began shortly before the archbishopric was established in 1152. The picture shows a contemporary view of the west front of the church.

trained as a priest stepped ashore on to Norwegian soil. He called himself Sverre, had grown up on the Faroes and maintained that he was a king's son. Sverre became the leader of an insurgent band who got the name *Birkebeiner* ("birch feet") because they were so poor that they had no proper footwear and made shoes from birch-bark.

Sverre and his men found themselves supported by several of Erling Skakke's enemies. In 1179 Erling was killed, and five years later Magnus, too, had to pay with his life. But this did not leave Sverre supreme in the land: his strongest opposition came from the church. During the 1190s the church together with a number of powerful men formed the *Bagler* party (from "bagall": a bishop's crozier).

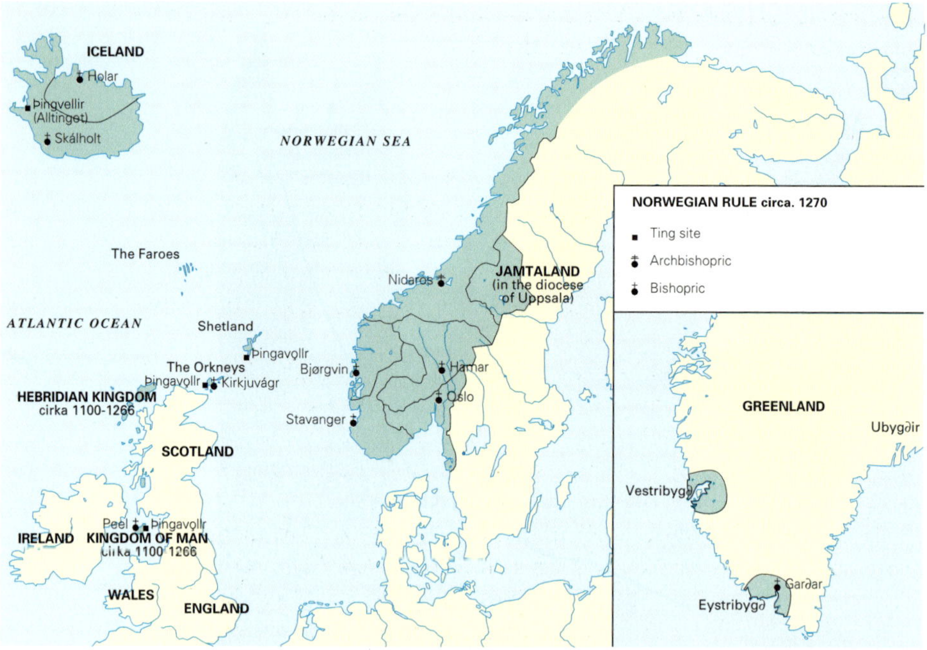
ICELAND
Holar
Þingvellir (Alltinget)
Skálholt
NORWEGIAN SEA
The Faroes
ATLANTIC OCEAN
Shetland
Þingavǫllr
The Orkneys
Þingavǫllr
Kirkjuvágr
HEBRIDIAN KINGDOM
cirka 1100-1266
SCOTLAND
IRELAND
Peel
Þingavǫllr
KINGDOM OF MAN
cirka 1100-1266
WALES
ENGLAND
Nidaros
JAMTALAND
(in the diocese of Uppsala)
Bjørgvin
Hamar
Oslo
Stavanger
NORWEGIAN RULE circa. 1270
Ting site
Archbishopric
Bishopric
GREENLAND
Ubygðir
Vestribygð
Garðar
Eystribygð

There were two main reasons why Sverre's conflict with the church was inevitable. In the first place, he challenged the crowned and anointed Magnus Erlingsson's monarchy. And secondly, accepting Sverre would destroy everything the church had gained in 1163. Sverre's struggle must however be viewed in a wider perspective. The demands for ecclesiastical freedom led to conflict between the clerical and temporal powers in several European countries, and Sverre's battle in Norway was part of a general European picture: the kings were fighting to regain and retain their influence over the church.

In the winter of 1202 Sverre lay dying in Bergen. At this time, the *Bagler* controlled the coast from Stad to Trondheimsfjord, the bishops had fled the country and Sverre had been excommunicated. Sverre advised his son to make peace with the church when he became king. Håkon followed this advice, and slowly Sverre's heirs and the church's leaders moved closer together. Despite this a *Birkebeiner* king and a *Bagler* king each ruled their own part of the country until 1217 when both died. The choice of king now fell on thirteen-year-old Håkon Håkonsson. His mother proved that he was Sverre's illegitimate grandson – she carried a red-hot iron bar to demonstrate his noble birth. She, like Gilchrist a century before, had God on her side. The young Håkon ruled alone.

The Norwegian Golden Age

Fully thirty years were to pass before Rome gave the illegitimate King its blessing, and it did not do it for nothing. Mollified by a considerable sum of money, the Pope closed his eyes to the fact that Håkon was illegitimate and promised that the King's descendants would be allowed to succeed him to the throne. And so inherited monarchy triumphed in Norway.

The 13th century is known as the "Golden Age" in Norwegian history. The Norwegian kings ruled over more territory than ever before. England was her principal trading partner, and Norwegian longships carried salted herring, dried fish and timber to English ports, returning with corn, but also woollen cloth, weapons and luxury goods.

Trade strengthened cultural influences. Norwegian craftsmen learnt how to build churches in England and France, and the castles that were raised, were on the French pattern, like Akershus Castle in Oslo and Vardøhus Fortress in Finnmark. French romances and adventures from the East were read aloud at the Norwegian court, and gradually these stories became more generally disseminated. Foreign styles coalesced with Norwegian archetypes, and the country got its own popular ballads in the Middle Ages. But the Norse produced their own great writersm, the most prominent of whom was the Icelander Snorre Sturlason who wrote the "Sagas of the Norwegian Kings" up to Sverre.

Towards the end of the 13th century Germans became Norway's most important trading partners. The population was increasing rapidly and the country had insufficient corn. But the German cities on the Baltic did, and their merchants' vessels proved better adapted to the corn traffic than the longships of the Norwegians. In the 14th century the King had to give merchants from Lübeck, Bremen and other members of the Hanseatic League special privileges. Bergen was their most important city, and here a German community of merchants and craftsmen burgeoned.

The royal governance of the High Middle Ages turned Norway into a state. Both locally and centrally the King set up an administrative apparatus on a nationwide scale. King Magnus the Lawmender promoted the enactment of laws for the entire country, based on the old regional laws. This *Landslov* was adopted at every common *ting*, which demonstrated that the King still paid attention to the farmers at the *ting*, although in reality the judicial authorities were now under royal control.

However, the King did not decide everything alone. To give his pronouncements greater force, he consulted noblemen and bishops. From the 1280s these "good men" functioned as a permanent Privy Council, for which the bishops, who knew Latin and were schooled in theology and law, were obvious candidates. Together with the King's local and central administration, the church's all-pervasive organisation held the state of Norway together.

Still, the Old Norwegian state stood on shifting sands. Håkon Håkonsson's law of succession of 1260 laid down that the King's eldest legitimate son should succeed to the throne. Håkon Magnusson (Håkon V) who reigned in the early 14th century, had no son, but his daughter Ingebjørg had married the Swedish Duke Erik of Södermanland. By him she had a son, Magnus. At Håkon V's deathbed in 1319 the country's leading men swore that no foreigner should have castle or fief in Norway and that the country would remain free. The dying King saw the threat that was looming.

Union and depopulation in the Late Middle Ages 1319–1537

When Håkon V died, three-year-old Magnus inherited the throne of Norway. In the same year he was elected King of Sweden, placing the realms within a personal union. In Norway, the Privy Council, which had now changed its name to the Council of State, was to rule together with the King's mother, Ingebjørg, until Magnus reached his majority. But both Ingebjørg and Magnus came into conflict with the Council. When Ingebjørg attempted to gain control of the Danish province of Skåne, the Council excluded her from power. Magnus continued Ingebjørg's policy from the time of his majority until he was removed from the throne in 1343.

The Swedish and Norwegian Councils of State forced the King to accept that his two sons would each inherit one realm as soon as they were grown up. The Councils were thus trying to repair the damage that joint sovereignty had left in its wake. But soon, an even greater catastrophe was to affect Norway. Icelandic chronicles relate that an English ship brought the plague to Bergen in the summer of 1349, but

Early in the 20th century the artist Theodor Kittelsen painted a series of pictures with motifs from the Black Death. Superstition had it that the plague travelled the country in the shape of an old hag who became known as "Pesta". If she carried a broom, everyone in the community would die; if she had a rake, a few would be spared.

Bergen was the largest and most important city in medieval Norway. There sprang up on its highly characteristic Bryggen waterfront a community of German merchants and craftsmen, and these Hanse got a monopoly on the dried fish trade from northern Norway.

other parts of the country were also affected at about the same time.

The infection spread rapidly. During the autumn and winter of 1349–50 the Black Death killed a third of the population. In the decades that followed the country was hit by other, more minor, epidemics until, by 1400, the population was half what it had been in the Golden Age.

The catastrophe of plague improved ordinary people's lives. After 1350, the farming families that had survived could take the best land, as whole communities had been laid waste, and accordingly, people moved away from the small farms. It was not until the 16th century that the reclamation of deserted farms began. Renting land got cheaper, and farmers paid less taxes and tithes. Taxes and tolls in 1500 were half what they had been in the Golden Age. Lack of labour meant that many switched to animal husbandry rather than cereal growing, and people ate a more protein rich diet than previously.

The state was not so fortunate. The loss of revenue weakened the King's administrative control. In rural communities, farmers themselves took over many functions. One example of this is the legal system. The ancient parochial court where the farmers themselves sat in judgement in private cases, underwent a revival.

The nobility was also enfeebled. Minor aristocratic families descended into the ranks of the farming community because the lands they owned produced less income. The higher reaches of the nobility who held fiefs from the King did better, for a weakened monarchy gave the rulers of such fiefdoms greater latitude. They fiefs of the Late Middle Ages were identical with the districts of the High Middle Ages; they were the cornerstones of the system that grew up were the royal castles under the command of a feudal lord. Within a considerable area around the castle, known as the *hovedlen*, the feudal lord could exercise authority on the King's behalf. But compared with the aristocracy in neighbouring countries, the Norwegian nobility was diminutive and unprosperous, and Swedes and Danes married into it.

The church did better. Though its revenues also fell, it was the country's biggest landowner. In the Late Middle Ages people's fear of death was greater than ever, and so they gave the church land for the good of their souls. The Archbishop of Nidaros became Norway's most powerful man and the natural leader of the Council of State. He received most of his tithe in the form of dried fish which he sold on to the Hanse merchants in Bergen.

Norway was subordinate to Sweden and Denmark whose populations were larger and agricultural areas many times bigger. Swedish and Danish nobility were also able to squeeze their farmers harder so that the loss of revenue was not so great. During the 14th and 15th centuries the Hanseatic League took control of Norwegian trade, and the fear of German economic and political advance grew in Scandinavia. The Kalmar Union has to be seen in this context.

In 1343 the Norwegian Council of State decided to adopt Magnus Eriksson's second son, Håkon, as king, and thus the personal union with Sweden was at an end. In 1363, King Håkon VI married Margrete, daughter of the Danish King Valdemar Atterdag. The marriage created a clash of interests with Sweden and the Swedish Council of State deposed Magnus Eriksson and elected Albrecht of Mecklenburg as king in his place. This initiated a struggle between two dynasties for power in Scandinavia.

Håkon VI and Margrete had a son, Olav, and on the death of Valdemar Atterdag in 1375 he was chosen as the Danish King. On his father's death in 1380, Olav inherited the Norwegian throne, and thus began the long period of union between Denmark and Norway that was to last right up until 1814.

When Olav IV died in 1387, Margrete managed to install her kinsman, Eric of Pomerania – a minor – as King of both Norway and Denmark. She attacked Sweden and deposed King Albrecht, and in 1397 the union of the three Scandinavian realms was sealed in the town of Kalmar. There, Eric of Pomerania was crowned King of Scandinavia, and Margrete personally ruled the three kingdoms.

Her policies were aimed at strengthening royal power at the expense of the Councils of State. Sweden and Norway were to be subjugated to the chief realm of Denmark. The Norwegian Council of State was not fully convened, and the state seal was removed to Copenhagen, the unified monarchy's royal seat. The Queen's supporters were given feudal lordships and bishoprics in Norway. Erik of Pomerania carried Margrete's anti-German policies even further, and this resulted in war with both the German princes and the Hanse during which German blockade and burdensome taxes affected Norway badly. Farmers revolted in Sweden and Norway, and in this situation the Swedish nobility were able to extricate the country from the union. But the Norwegian Council of State was too weak to revive a separate Norwegian kingdom.

In 1513 Christian II became King of Denmark and Norway. The Norwegian Council of State was disregarded, the King turned commoners who supported him into feudal lords, and his private secretary was made Archbishop of Nidaros. Christian wanted to revive the Kalmar Union, and he did conquer Sweden, but that was the beginning of the end. After the coronation in Stockholm in 1520, he murdered 82 nobles and clergymen as a warning to others, provoking rebellions against "Christian the tyrant" among the Swedish and Danish aristocracies, and in 1523 he fled to the Low Countries.

Norway had remained outside this conflict, but at this point a powerful politician, Olav Englebrektsson, took over the bishop's seat in Nidaros. By this time, Martin Luther's doctrine was well known in Denmark, and the archbishop realised that soon it might become a threat to the Catholic Church in Norway. As the head of the Council of State Olav did everything possible to keep the country free from "the Lutheran poison". But he did not succeed. An alliance with the German Emperor and the exiled Christian II ended in failure. The archbishop had to flee to the Netherlands as well, and in 1537 Christian III's forces reached Norway. The newly chosen King was a Lutheran and had brought the Reformation to Denmark the previous year. Now he was demanding the throne of Norway.

Queen Margrete's face on her sarcophagus in Roskilde Cathedral in Denmark.

Norway in a union with Denmark

1537–1814

"Under Denmark's crown for ever"

As early as 1536 Norway's fate had been sealed. That autumn Duke Christian had won Denmark with his lancers, and as Christian III he brought in the Reformation. The coronation charter he negotiated with the Danish Council of State, prior to his election as king, stated that Norway was so weakened that it could not remain an independent realm but should become "a part of Denmark's realm and under Denmark's crown for ever".

After the Catholic Church's defeat the small Norwegian aristocracy was too weak to maintain the country's independence. From now on Norway was ruled from Copenhagen where the King and his Council of State of nobles shared power. When the King died, the Council of State elected a new one, who automatically became the King of Norway too. The Norwegian Council of State had gone for good.

But the Norwegian nation lived on in customs and dialects, even though its written language became Danish. The people felt themselves to be Norwegian, and the kings called themselves Kings of Denmark *and* Norway.

Norway, the Reformation and royal power 1537–1660

The Reformation strengthened royal power. Now the church's leader was the King in Copenhagen and not the pope in Rome. There had been no Lutheran stirrings in Norway as there had been

Christian IV ascended the throne as an eleven-year-old, and took the reigns of power when he reached his majority in 1596. This portrait was painted by Pieter Isaacsz just after the Kalmar War (1611-13), during which the king made gains. Christian is wearing a field marshall's sash.

in Denmark, and Norwegians just had to accept the new doctrine without question. It must have seemed strange that relics, monasteries and the worship of saints disappeared, and that a conspicuous part of the new church service was a sermon in Danish.

But it took time to recruit qualified priests, and many of those chosen in the first years after the Reformation were unenlightened and argumentative. Despite this, the priesthood gradually became a useful tool of the state: from the pulpit they could plead the King's case "to the rude and ignorant masses".

The Reformation also had an economic aspect. While prior to 1537 the Catholic Church had been the biggest landowner with more than 40% of the land, everything now became the King's. The church's gold and silver treasures were sent to Copenhagen to be melted down. In 1540 a total of 125 kilos of gold and silver were shipped from Trondheim to Copenhagen, including Saint Olav's casket.

The King bolstered his power in other ways as well. Norway was divided up into five main provinces and a number of subsidiary ones, and these were generally granted to Danish nobles by the King. At the start of this period the provincial governor had responsibility for most administrative functions, but gradually the King increased his power at the expense of the provincial nobility. Historians speak of a shift from aristocratic provincial governance to royal administration in the decades prior to 1660. From the end of the 16th century provincial governors had to provide proper accounts. Moreover, the bailiff, who had originally been the provincial governor's personal servant, became a royal official. It was the bailiffs who collected taxes and who had responsibility for peace and order within their districts.

In the century after 1537, the need for professionalism grew steadily as society grew more complicated. One of the provincial governor's duties had been to command soldiers in war, but from the 1620s the King began to employ military officers. And so, professional soldiers began to lead Norwegian peasant armies. The need for control and professionalism can also be seen in the legal system. The *sorenskriver*, who originally had been no more than the farmers' secretary in the parochial court, quickly became an independent judge of the crown. Throughout the period excise tariffs rose sharply due to increased timber exports, and, from 1632, the King set up a dedicated customs service an thus took another duty away from provincial governors. Finally the King appointed a governor-general

A 17th century painted glass pane showing women boiling potions, from Årdal in Sogn. The knowledge of such "wise women" was very much in demand in the old days, but it was also feared. The period between 1570 and 1670 was the age of the witch-hunt in Norway, and we know of two thousand prosecutions. Five hundred people were burnt at the stake, most of them female paupers.

(*Stattholder*) for Norway in 1572. His residence was at Akershus Castle and he was the King's chief representative. The appointment shows that the King wanted greater control and, more than anything else, that he regarded Norway as a separate realm.

Of all the kings that reigned in the century after the Reformation, Christian IV (1588–1648) stands out. He was the "king who discov-

TRONDHEIM'S LEN
Trondheim
JEMTLAND
HERJEDALEN
FINLAND
KEKSHOLM'S LEN
RUSSLAND
S W E D E N
Bergen
Kristiania
Stockholm
Reval
INGERMAN-LAND
DANO-NORWEGIAN KINGDOM
BÅHUSLEN
Gothenburg
LIVONIA
Riga
NORTH SEA
HALLAND
SKÅNE
BLEKINGE
THE BALTIC
Copenhagen
Bornholm
SWEDISH POMERANIA
EAST PRUSSIA
POLAND
BREMEN
Bremen
PRUSSIA

ered Norway". He had great faith in the possibilities of the
Norwegian mountains and forests, and he visited the country no less
than thirty times. He also harboured great expectations of Norway as
a military resource. But Christian IV died a broken man. His foreign
policy had gone awry and the Crown Prince had died a year before
his father. The Council of State elected his younger son, Frederik, to
the throne, and he had to acquiesce to a tough coronation charter
that secured the Council of State's power and the privileges of the
aristocracy. However, twelve years later Frederik III was to win a
crushing victory over the Council of State and the aristocracy.
Scandinavian politics may provide the clue as to why Christian suffered defeat and Frederik triumphed.

The fight for supremacy in Scandinavia

In the early part of the 17th century, Denmark-Norway had the upper hand over its arch-enemy Sweden. A glance at the map shows why. The area at the mouth of the River Göta was the Swedes' only outlet to the North Sea, and the Danish King controlled Øresund where he levied excise tariffs. Naval supplies from the Baltic countries – linen, hemp, tar, pitch and timber – passed through this Kronborg bottle-neck. The sea-going powers of England and the Netherlands were dependent on these materials, and so Øresund became an international focus of attention On the other hand, the borders in the north were not fixed; Norwegians, Swedes and Russians all demanded taxes from the Sami. Accordingly, it became Sweden's object to gain supremacy in the north and fight its way out of the Dano-Norwegian manacle.

During the Kalmar War (1611–13), Christian IV attempted to stop the Swedish advance in the Baltic and in the north, and he demanded the conscription of a peasant army of 8,000 men from Norway. But the Norwegian performance was pitiable. The Danish provincial governors had little experience as officers and the peasant soldiers lacked food and enough firearms. Many drank, fought, and fired their weapons indiscriminately, and their officers were unable to prevent mass desertions.

Despite this, the Kalmar War ended well for Christian IV. The peace accord stipulated that the coast between Tysfjord and Varanger was Norwegian. The efforts of the joint fleet and the Danish battle on Swedish territory saw to that. But the war did show one thing regarding Norway as a military resource: it was *possible* to raise a large peasant army.

Against the will of the Council of State, Christian IV threw himself into the Thirty Years War (1618–48) in Germany on the Protestant side. In 1625 he declared war in his role as a German duke, but the King suffered humiliating defeats, and he was only just able to keep his kingdoms intact at the peace four years later. The Swedes fared better and won considerable victories on German soil.

The war was felt by the people of Norway, too. More than 3,000 Norwegians had been drafted into service in the joint fleet, and the border fortresses were given permanent garrisons totalling 350 men. In 1628 the King proclaimed a statute of war for Norway and thus laid the foundations of the Norwegian army. The country was divided into units called a *legd*, containing four full farms each, and each *legd* was duty bound to supply and equip one soldier. The system could supply more than 6,000 infantrymen, but because the peace came in 1629, its implementation was delayed. However, the pattern for future civil defence had been laid.

Christian IV was not inactive in the years that followed. It was especially important to increase receipts, and to achieve this, he increased the Øresund tariffs, but this brought Sweden and the Netherlands together in 1640. The fortunes of war in Germany had given Sweden a place amongst the great powers of Europe. This was the situation when the Danish nobleman, Hannibal Sehested, arrived in Norway as Governor-General in 1642. He was the King's son-in-law, a trusted man, and despite his youth – he was only 34 – he was a diplomat of experience and linguistic ability. It fell to him to oversee the construction of the army. The edicts of 1628 were to be put into practice, and at the same time the aristocracy, the priesthood and the wealthiest farmers were ordered to supply 520 armed horsemen and their mounts. Hannibal Sehested negotiated with the burghers the equipping of *ships of defence*, merchantmen which could be used in sea battles if necessary. He also got officers and weapons from abroad. All this made for even heavier taxes on the peasantry. Never before had the authorities asked so much of them.

Just before Christmas 1643, well trained Swedish troops marched up through Jutland, which they quickly occupied. Christian IV gathered his forces for battle in the rest of the realm. Hannibal Sehested's Norwegian army won no great victories, but Norwegian troops carried out a number of skirmishes across the border in southern Norway, thus tying up a number of Swedish troops. Despite better organisation, the soldiers were still unreliable and many went home. We know of examples of farmers on both sides of the border making pacts to leave each other alone! Most people probably felt that it was not their war, but the Governor-General's, and appositely enough it has become known as "Hannibal's Feud". "The Norwegian pony cannot be relied on in a tight spot," the Governor-General complained. At the peace of 1645, the King had to cede the islands of Gotland and Øsel together with the Norwegian provinces of Jemtland and Herjedalen, while the Netherlands paid reduced duties at Øresund.

The revenge war waged by Frederik III in 1657–60 was also a catastrophe. Norway lost Båhuslen, while Denmark had to cede its provinces to the east of Øresund. This despite a good Norwegian showing and the temporary retaking of Jemtland. For the first time Norway had made a sizeable contribution to the defence of the joint

realm, but in 1660 Sweden's place as the great power in Scandinavia was indisputable.

Denmark-Norway had borrowed money for the wars from the burghers of Copenhagen, and after the peace of 1660 the monarchy was facing an acute financial crisis. It was left to Frederik III to solve the problems.

Norway and absolutism

After the Reformation, the aristocracy's might was gradually weakened, and the wars showed that the provincial aristocracy was poorly equipped to lead soldiers in battle. But it was the economic crisis of 1660 that finished them for good. At a meeting of the Estates in Copenhagen that autumn, the King aligned himself with the Danish burghers who were thirsting for power. At the meeting the nobility agreed to pay taxes, but to prevent onslaughts on other aristocratic privileges, it made major tax proposals that affected the other Estates. After tense negotiations between the burghers and the clergy on one side and the nobility on the other, the King imprisoned the Council of State and the nobility in a hostile Copenhagen until they gave way. Frederik III then had the coronation charter guaranteeing the nobility's privileges returned to him, and he and his successors got heredi-

A "rose-painted" interior from Rygistua in Telemark, painted by Ola Hansson in 1782. "Rose painting" was a decorative rural art form that developed during the 18th and 19th centuries. It drew its inspiration from urban craftwork circles and 17th century church decoration. During the 17th century a number of rural church interiors were decorated with Renaissance acanthus vines and flowers. Subsequent European styles, especially the baroque and rococo, also inspired Norwegian country artists.

The christianisation of the Sami began in Norway at the start of the 18th century, and their old nature worship gradually declined. The illustration shows a Sami with a magic drum used for contacting these natural gods. During christianisation, hundreds of such magic drums were burnt.

tary rights to the throne. The Council of State was dissolved, and all power fell to the King. His power had become absolute.

Norway was away from the centre of events in the autumn of 1660, and Norwegians were not represented at the allegiance ceremony in Copenhagen in October. But the following year there was a special allegiance ceremony in Kristiania (Oslo), although the monarchy had always viewed Norway as a hereditary kingdom. Frederik III was represented by his son, Prince Christian. Of the 543 representatives of the Estates, as many as 408 were farmers. This shows the special position Norwegian farmers occupied in contrast to their Danish counterparts: a mere handful of farmers took part in Copenhagen, and only one was allowed to kiss the King's hand.

After 1660 both the central and local administrative systems were reorganised. Prior to 1660 the kingdoms had had one office for matters of state, but now a system was introduced rather similar to our modern departments, where matters were divided up according to subject. These colleges also contained representatives of the bourgeoisie, which goes to demonstrate that the nobility had lost its monopoly on power.

The King also ordered a new administrative structure in which the fiefs were replaced by counties (*amt*), which were put in the charge of salaried *amtmenn*, or district governors. The counties were further sub-divided into bailiwicks (*fogderier*). The King did not want the district governors to become too powerful, and so military officials were employed to lead the army. All officials were appointed by the King and there were about 1,600 of them in Norway during the period of absolutism. They comprised district governors, judges, bailiffs, priests, officers and customs men. Local government was headed by the colleges in Copenhagen, and above them again was the absolute monarch and his counsellors. But the road to the capital was long, and when a matter needed to be examined and decided, the pronouncements of Norwegian officials were given great weight. It was also to prove that a large number of initiatives came from the local administration or the people of Norway.

Peasant society

In the period between 1500 and 1800 the population of Norway increased from about 150,000 to 900,000, and nine out of ten people were connected to the land. The reason that numbers rose was that plagues were absent, but the mortality rate was still high, especially amongst children. As late as the 18th century, nearly a quarter of all infants died in their first year of life.

Housing remained poor, and though a number of farms in eastern Norway had built two storey farmhouses prior to 1660, it was still dominated by the draughty log houses with central fireplaces we know from medieval times. The diet was simple; for most the daily ration was porridge, gruel and various types of flatbread. There was no health service to cure or prevent disease. This kind of society was an easy prey to epidemics and starvation, and bad years or empty seas could have catastrophic consequences. But despite these setbacks numbers rose, and in the 18th century the population pressure began to be felt.

From the end of the 17th century Norwegian farmers began to get proprietorial rights over the land they worked. When absolutism arrived in 1660, only 20% of farming land was in the hands of farmers, but by 1800 the majority of Norwegian farming families lived on their own land. To pay off the national debt caused by the wars against Sweden, King Frederik III had given land to the burghers to whom he owed money, but they quickly sold it on to the farmers against a mortgage in their farms. Thus the burghers freed up capital which they could invest in other industries, like shipping and mining, and the farmers were keen to buy. The proprietorship of land provided security and the right to free felling in forest belonging to the farm, enabling farmes to pay off their mortage. Only in the north of the country did landlords hold back on account of the hunting and fishing rights that went with the farms.

The increase in population after 1500 required more employment. During the first century the deserted farms from the Late Middle Ages were reclaimed, and throughout the country farms were divided if they were large enough. However, this was not enough, and the result was that a large underclass of smallholders (*husmenn*) grew up in rural districts after 1660. A smallholder's family would be allowed to clear a small croft on a farm. The family had to pay rent for this holding. In eastern Norway and in Trøndelag there were often many smallholdings on each farm because there was a large demand for labour in the forests and on the land, and the whole family would help with the work. Contracts were all but unknown, the smallholder's family lived at the mercy of the farmer, and many were evicted as they became old or ill. There were fewer smallholders in western Norway, and they occupied a higher social position. The need for labour was not so great, and the payment in labour was therefore minimal. In this part of the country smallholders lived by fishing and plying a trade. The numbers of smallholders grew from 17,000 in the 17th century to 48,000 in 1800.

What demands did the state make of farmers during the period of absolutism? Naturally, they were obliged to pay taxes on the land they worked. But Norway became a low tax country compared with Denmark. Time and again the authorities attempted to increase taxes, but they had to give up. To take the Skåne War (1676–79) as an example: in the years preceding the hostilities there had been crop failures over the entire country. At the same time, defence demands had been increased. Now two full farms were responsible for equipping one soldier, whereas in 1628 that duty had been shared between four. During this war of revenge, the King's step-brother, Governor-General Ulrik Frederik Gyldenløve (1638–1704) led the Norwegian army to notable victories over the Swedes, and even though Denmark-Norway gained no territory, the war demonstrated that the Norwegian army was every bit as important as the joint fleet and the professional troops in Denmark. During the war the tax conundrum was pushed to the fore. Should more taxes be squeezed out of the Norwegians? Gyldenløve thought not. Nobody was to be allowed to destroy the fighting spirit of his effective army, and the King gave in. He could not ignore a population with military training and an aggressive Sweden, so the taxation system of the 1600s remained in force until well into the 19th century. Furthermore, the tax-paying farmers profited from inflation, which had the effect of lessening the effect of the taxes. In the second half of the 18th century, the Norwegian farmer lost between 4 and 10% of his gross income in taxes and tithes. In France, a farmer had to part with 60 to 75%.

Similar trends can be found in other areas. During the 1730s the problem of beggars forced the implementation of a more effective system of poor relief; and confirmation, introduced in 1736, required children to be able to read. Farmers had the financial responsibility for poor relief and board-schools, but poor relief was of little use to most of the poor, and for the remainder of the period of absolutism the schools were in a wretched state. In reality, the state had little leverage on farmers, and rural society was too poor to be able to care properly for those who needed it most.

Towns and middle-class trades

In the 17th and 18th centuries most countries in Europe pursued a mercantile trade policy, and Denmark-Norway was no exception. The authorities wanted to encourage economic life with import regulations, protective tariffs and monopolies, so that the state could grow strong and be as self-sufficient as possible. Civil society had a key role in this policy, as demonstrated by town charters of 1667. These laws gave the burghers a monopoly on trade and craftwork throughout the country, and it was only at the end of the period of absolutism that the King eased this burgher-friendly mercantile policy.

The timber trade became a major industry in the 17th century. The water-driven gate saw made it possible to produce boards and planks, the form of timber most in demand in Europe. The most

The furnace house at Bærum Works, painted by C.A. Lorentzen in 1790. This iron foundry, founded in 1610, was one of the first of its kind in Norway. The fire can be seen surging out of the blast furnace where the ore was smelted.

Scandinavia's largest wooden building, the Stiftsgård (*The Residence*) in Trondheim, was built by Cecilia Christine de Scholler in the 1770s. The house got its name when the state turned it into a residence for the diocesan governor (*stift-amtmannen*) in 1800. Since 1906 the building has been the monarch's royal residence in Trondheim.

important market was England, and despite attempts by the authorities to regulate the export to prevent deforestation, the trade increased. Both farmers and smallholders profited from timber sales, forestry work and carting, but it was the wealthiest bourgeoisie – the mercantile aristocracy – that made the greatest profit. In 1688 the King decreed that a large number of sawmills were to be shut down to increase the price of timber and to prevent deforestation, and each remaining saw was to have a quota. This affected farmers because it was the smallest sawmills that stopped turning, and they were thus pushed out of the most lucrative of their production chains. By the middle of the 18th century the mercantile aristocracy comprised a handful of timber merchants in the timber exporting ports.

The mining industry was also lucrative for the mercantile aristocracy. In the 16th century Norway had few mines and quarries, but the 17th century saw a huge period of expansion, with King Christian IV as a powerful motive force. Self-sufficiency and large resources of precious metals made good economic sense, and the wars with Sweden were a drain on finances. So the King put his trust in the Norwegian mountains. He brought in mining experts from Germany, and a number of mines were operating at a profit as early as 1660. Kongsberg silver-works and Røros copper-works are good examples.

In the 17th and 18th centuries two out of every five of the population lived in areas where fishing was an important industry. Most fishing families ran a farm, but in the west and in Trøndelag, and above all in northern Norway, fishing provided considerable additional income on farms. It was the big seasonal fisheries, especially in Lofoten, that provided income. In 1800, 15,000 men took part in this fishing, and Bergen and Trondheim were centres for the export of fish to Central and Southern Europe.

From ancient times cod had been dried on racks. It was a cheap method of preservation that the fisherman could manage on his own, and the north had very stable wind drying conditions. From about 1700 it became the norm to add salting to the cod-drying process, and this *klippfisk* production was most prevalent in southern Norway. It was facilitated by cheap salt from Southern Europe, but this type of preservation turned the fisherman into a mere supplier of raw materials. It required capital to buy salt, and only the merchants had capital.

The growth of Norwegian shipping must be viewed in the light of the increase in industry. Though Norway boasted a significant volume of exports right back to the Middle Ages, it had been transported in foreign vessels dominated by the Hanse, the Dutch, the British and the Danes. Using mercantile principles the authorities in the 17th century tried to stimulate Norwegian shipping. One example is the *ships of defence* which were granted excise relief. The British Navigation Acts had some effect as they precluded competitors from the cargo transport between Norway and Britain, but it was during the European wars towards the end of the 17th century that Norwegian ships got their chance, and the period from 1690 to 1710 has been called the "first golden age" of Norwegian shipping. Denmark-Norway kept neutral, but after King Frederik IV took the kingdoms into the Great Scandinavian War in 1709, things began to go wrong. After the peace of 1720, foreigners had again taken the initiative. It was not until the revolutionary wars of the second half of the 18th century that Norwegian shipowners got another chance. Once again, neutrality proved profitable, and by the time the kingdoms were drawn into the Napoleonic Wars in 1807, Norway had become one of Europe's greatest seafaring nations.

City growth and the increase in trade are closely linked. At the time a town was called a *kjøpstad*, and in 1660 only eight towns had this status. By 1800 there were twenty-three of them in Norway. The medieval towns were still the most important: Bergen with its mid-18th century tally of 14,000 inhabitants was twice as large as the similarly sized Kristiania and Trondheim put together.

Stability and growth in the 18th century

The first twenty years of the 18th century saw unrest in Scandinavia. The Great Scandinavian War broke out in 1700, but Denmark-Norway only seriously took up arms in 1709. Sweden's young warrior king, Carl XII had, after a number of victories, suffered a severe defeat near Poltava in the Ukraine, and now King Frederik IV acted to win back old Dano-Norwegian territory. He attacked Skåne, but the campaign failed, and Carl returned to the offensive. In 1716 and 1718 the Swedes penetrated southern Norway. During the siege of Halden in December 1718, King Carl XII was killed. A Norwegian or Swedish bullet put a stop to the warrior's career.

The war cost both realms dear. Amongst other things, the citizenry of Halden had set light to 330 houses to halt the enemy. Sweden had to relinquish its freedom from duty in Øresund, and all its possessions in the Baltic and Germany were lost. Denmark-Norway did not win back any land, but Sweden's age of greatness was over and the balance of power was restored.

The aim of the absolutist monarchs was to weld the realms together into an economic, political and cultural entity with Copenhagen at its centre. The results of this United Monarchy policy were patently obvious by the latter half of the 18th century when between half and two thirds of the Norway's audited national income was transferred to Denmark. Every part of the administration in Norway was directly under the control of the central administration in Copenhagen, and Norway was ruled as if it was a collection of counties, rather than a separate kingdom. While Copenhagen expanded as a centre for politics, trade, art and science, Kristiania remained a backwater.

But the authorities listened to the advice coming from Norwegian officials, and most Norwegians did not feel oppressed. Throughout the entire union with Denmark, Norway had its own legal code and proprietorial rights were enshrined in law. Legal accountability was the order of the day, and both high and low had the right to have their case brought before the King by making a petition as it was then called. The peasantry trusted that the King, who was almost a father

figure, would cut through the red tape and give the people their rights.

"The Haugians" painted by Adolph Tidemand in 1852.

But of course there were rifts. For the last twenty years of the 18th century the farmer Christian Jensen Lofthus (1750–97) and the preacher Hans Nielsen Hauge (1771–1824), each in their own field, fought battles with the authorities. Lofthus complained to the King that officials in Agder were bleeding farmers dry and that town dwellers were using their privileges to drive farmers off their land. He became the leader of a sizeable peasant uprising. For eleven years he sat chained to a rock in Akershus Castle, and he died there in 1797. It was not until two years later that his life sentence was confirmed by the Supreme Court. However, the demands Lofthus had made were taken seriously by the authorities; officials were dismissed and the regulations changed. Hans Nielsen Hauge fought

Eilif Petersen called this work from 1892 "An Evening at the the Norwegian Society, 1780". Johan Nordal Brun is reading poetry while Johan Herman Wessel raises his glass of punch. The proprietress, Madame Juel, is bringing in more refreshments.

for the right to preach the word of God freely, a monopoly then enjoyed by priests of the state church. His band of supporters grew rapidly to become a nationwide folk movement. Hauge, too, was imprisoned for years without sentence, but the movement he had created could not be destroyed.

The bourgeoisie and official classes criticised centralisation, and Copenhagen was compared with a blood-sucking leech. Demands for a Norwegian bank and university were raised several times, but the King refused, fearing that the United Monarchy would be destroyed. The upper classes kept abreast of what was going on in Europe, and it is hardly surprising that patriotism blossomed in these circles. National identity also found expression at the Norwegian Society in Copenhagen which was a meeting place for authors and students from Norway. John Nordahl Brun's battle song "To Norway, birthplace of giants" shows that in such circles Norwegian sentiment was well nurtured.

But sentiment and dawning nationalism aside, there was little danger that Denmark and Norway would go their separate ways during the 18th century. During the 1790s the government took a liberal line, and a number of measures stilled the criticism of the bourgeoisie. The buoyant times around the turn of the century dispelled the discontent of the middle classes still further. It was only when the kingdoms got drawn into the Napoleonic Wars that cracks in the union began to appear.

Even so, Norway was in quite a different position towards the end of the 18th century than when it had been "a part of Denmark's realm" in 1536. The growth in population and economic life had given the country financial strength, and there was relatively little social injustice. The absolute monarchy had fostered a cultural and economic elite of officials and burghers, and the fact that Norway had been regarded as a kingdom even after 1537, was to make it easier to rebuild a Norwegian state in 1814.

1814

Independence and new union

When the year 1814 dawned, the union between Denmark and Norway was still intact, and was ruled over by an absolute monarch. During the course of a few hectic summer months Norway became an independent realm with its own king and a constitution based on the sovereignty of the people. In the autumn the country was forced into a new union – this time with Sweden.

Denmark-Norway chooses Napoleon

In 1792 France declared war on Austria and Prussia, and from now on war was to rage in Europe right up until 1814. Denmark-Norway managed, by a careful balancing act, to keep itself neutral. The union exploited the economic conditions of war, and the middle classes in Norway made a lot of money. At the time there was talk of a "golden age" for shipping and the export industries.

But it was hard not to get sucked in as Country after country had to choose one of the two principal antagonists – Emperor Napoleon Bonaparte in France or the naval power Britain. The British wanted to prevent neutral ships carrying goods to France, and British warships rummaged Dano-Norwegian merchant vessels. To protect his trade the King sent the ships in convoy accompanied by warships. This provocative policy caused a British fleet to attack Copenhagen in 1801, and after a short and bloody battle the British forced Denmark-Norway to give up convoys. From then on British warships were free to inspect the cargoes of Dano-Norwegian merchantmen.

In September 1807 Britain attacked again. Soldiers were landed

The Constitutional Assembly at Eidsvoll, painted by Oscar Wergeland in 1855. The painting now hangs behind the rostrum of the *Storting*. The independence faction's leader, Christian Magnus Falsen, is standing by the table. Seated on his right is the secretary of the assembly, Wilhelm F.K. Christie. Between them, on the opposite side of the table, is the seated figure of Count Herman Wedel Jarlsberg.

on Zealand, and warships bombarded Copenhagen. The British took away most of the Dano-Norwegian fleet, a total of 37 large vessels and several smaller ones, because they feared they could fall into Napoleon's hands. For Denmark-Norway this was the end of a hundred years of peace. Eleven days after the so-called "filching of the fleet" King Frederik VI chose to ally himself with Napoleon. But this proved a fateful decision for Norway because the union committed itself to joining the blockade of Britain. The King had deflected Napoleon from attacking Denmark and his dukedoms in Schleswig-Holstein, but for Norway the agreement meant that the country got no supplies from abroad.

War and blockade

Once war with Britain was a fact, Norway was in difficulties because the British prevented Norwegian ships from carrying timber, fish and iron to foreign ports. Norway was dependent on corn from Denmark, but even this trade was seriously reduced. In this situation the King was forced to give up the policy of a United Monarchy. He set up a Government Commission in Kristiania which was to run the country during the blockade. Norway was completely isolated when Denmark-Norway and Sweden went to war in 1808. Earlier that year, Russia had taken Finland from Sweden, and the Swedish King, Gustav IV, wanted to conquer Norway as compensation for his loss. But things did not go according to the King's plans. The Norwegian peasant soldiers defended themselves well and beat the Swedes in several minor battles in southern Norway. At the end of the year the parties entered a cease-fire, and with the peace of 1809 everything was back to normal between the two realms.

The Swedes were discontented with their king. The loss of Finland and the unsuccessful Norwegian campaign forced Gustav IV to abdicate. His old, childless uncle was chosen as the new king under the title Carl XIII, and it was obvious Sweden needed an effective heir to the throne. The choice fell on one of Napoleon's generals, Jean Baptiste Bernadotte. He arrived in Sweden as the Crown Prince in 1810 and took the name Carl Johan. From then on the Crown Prince was Sweden's uncontested leader, and his aim was to conquer Norway.

Both the bourgeoisie and the common people suffered badly after the filching of the fleet in 1807. The timber trade and fish exports suf-

fered. Worst afflicted was the eastern region of the country which was dependent on corn supplies from Denmark. "All that is heard here is cries for corn and food," one merchant wrote in May 1809.

On several occasions the Government Commission in Norway had demanded that the King alter his foreign policy. Nevertheless, Frederik VI kept to his alliance with Napoleon and the blockade of Britain. But by the summer of 1809 even the King saw that the discontent in Norway could rupture the union. So he allowed Norway to resume timber sales to Britain, provided the British allowed corn traffic to sail unhindered between Norway and Denmark. This "licence trade" saved the Norwegian bourgeoisie from ruin and the people in the east of the country from starvation. The crisis was over for the moment.

In 1812 Napoleon attacked his old ally, Russia. Because the war had escalated, Frederik VI was forced to give up the licence trade. In the east of Norway the summer was particularly cold that year, and the crops minimal. In the north of the country the fishing failed and the corn froze. There was poverty and hunger all across the land, and

The British frigate *Tartar* took part in the blockade of Norway. Here it is seen joining battle with Norwegian gunboats just off the gunpowder works at Alvøen near Bergen in 1808.

death was a constant companion. The peasants rose in several places, but just as in the days of Lofthus and Hauge they reserved their spleen for merchants and officials, and not the King and his foreign policy.

Napoleon's defeat in Russia was the beginning of the end for the emperor and for the Dano-Norwegian United Monarchy. Sweden joined Napoleon's enemies, and the great powers promised Carl Johan Norway if he helped defeat France. After the victory at the Battle of Leipzig in 1813, Carl Johan broke away and marched against Denmark. After a short war, Frederik VI was forced to surrender and on 14 January 1814 he signed the Peace of Kiel. By its terms he ceded Norway to the King of Sweden. The 434-year-old union of Denmark and Norway was over.

Prince Christian Frederik and the Constitution

When the news of the Peace of Kiel reached Norway, the country had an obvious leader. He was the Dano-Norwegian heir apparent, Prince Christian Frederik, who the King had appointed governor-general in the spring of 1813. The Prince was only 26 years old and had no administrative or military experience, but he was gifted, hard-working, personable and charming. His most important task was to secure the union with Denmark for Frederik VI and himself.

Christian Frederik refused to accept the Peace of Kiel, and he immediately set to work strengthening his own position in Norway. Officially, Frederik VI was opposed to this. He was bound by the treaty he had signed in Kiel, but secretly he supported the Crown Prince's plans. Perhaps the Norwegian crown was not lost after all! A few days after the Peace of Kiel was signed, the King covertly allowed corn ships to set sail for Norway. It was imperative the Swedes and the British did not find out about the double game he was playing.

Christian Frederik's greatest antagonist in Norway was Count Herman Wedel-Jarlsberg (1779–1840) had worked towards bringing Norway into a union with Sweden during the blockade and the years of privation. He maintained that only a permanent peace with the Swedes and the British could secure foreign trade and corn supplies, and so a union with Sweden would be good for patrician and peasant alike. However, Wedel-Jarlsberg and his supporters did want Norway to be a separate nation, and thought that a king shared with Sweden should not prevent extensive Norwegian autonomy.

Jean Baptiste Bernadotte was a lawyer's son from Pau in southern France. In Napoleon's service he rose to become Marshall of France and Prince of Ponte Corvo in Italy. In 1810 he was elected Crown Prince of Sweden under the name Carl Johan and adopted by King Carl XIII. This canvas, painted by Caroline Cathinca Engelhardt in 1875, now hangs in the Stiftsgård in Trondheim.

Christian Frederik's line prevailed, however. The ties to Denmark were still strong, and the Prince controlled Norway's national administration with its loyal officials. Despite the attempts of Carl Johan's agents to sway the Norwegians, the Prince's propaganda was more effective. He spoke and wrote of "his beloved Norwegian people" and of Norway's "prosperity and glory". At the end of January he travelled to Trondheim from Kristiania to win support, and wrote in his diary: "I spoke to the people at every opportunity, and assured them that I would not fail them, that Norway could, and should, defend itself by means of its sons' courage." The Prince was playing on the fear of coming under "the Swedish yoke".

On 16 February 1814, Christian Frederik assembled twenty-one of the country's leading citizens and officials for a meeting at Eidsvoll. This "meeting of the great" was to assess the Prince's demands. Christian Frederik claimed the Norwegian throne by right of succession, and wanted absolute power in accordance with the Norwegian Monarchy Act of 1661. But the great men had other thoughts. They wanted a liberal constitution, and a new king had to be chosen by the people. It was abundantly obvious that the Prince was the natural choice, but he had to accept that he took his regal power from the people.

And Christian Frederik acceded to these demands. The Prince knew only too well that the Norwegian officials and bourgeoisie had been influenced by the ideals of freedom in the Napoleonic and revolutionary age, and that it would be unwise to provoke powerful men in his present, difficult situation. So Christian Frederik and the great men together decided that the people should elect representatives to a meeting at Eidsvoll that would write the Constitution. They also decided that the electors and the elected should take a "people's oath" that they would work for Norwegian independence. Christian Frederik would rule the country as regent in the interim.

Christian Frederik was the son of heir presumptive Prince Frederik and Sophie Frederikke of Mecklenburg-Schwerin. His cousin King Frederik VI, eighteen years his senior, had no surviving sons. And so Christian Frederik succeeded him on the throne. The painting is by J.L. Lund, 1813.

At the beginning of April the first representatives arrived at Eidsvoll. On Easter Sunday, 10 April, the Prince Regent and the people's representatives met for communion and the following day Christian Frederik opened the Constitutional Assembly. There was a total of 112 representatives – 18 businessmen, 37 farmers and 57 civil and military officials. The Prince did not himself take part in the meetings, but he lived at Eidsvoll and influenced the decisions taken. He did have the opportunity of making representations; he could refuse to accept the throne if the Constitution was not to his liking.

The Constitutional Assembly divided into two parties. The independence party, by far the largest, supported Christian Frederik's policies and its leader, Chief Magistrate Christian Magnus Falsen (1782–1830), was loyal to the Prince Regent. The union party's leader was Count Wedel-Jarlsberg and most of his supporters came from the upper middle classes. They believed that Norway could not disregard the Peace of Kiel, and that an accommodation with Sweden was therefore inevitable.

The men at Eidsvoll took six weeks to draft a constitution for Norway. They modelled it on several constitutions that had been forged during the Napoleonic and revolutionary age, but it was the French one of 1791 which had the greatest influence. It had already been translated into Norwegian by the time the Constitutional Assembly began work.

The sovereignty of the people was the backbone of the Constitution that was drafted. Power was shared between the *Storting* (the National Assembly), the courts and the King on Montesquieu's principle, but one of its characteristics was that the King was given a lot of power. He was the supreme military leader and he could declare war and make peace. He was also able to raise taxes and appoint officials and he had a suspensive veto on legislation. The *Storting's* duties were to make laws and grant monies, but it was only to meet for three months every three years unless the King decreed otherwise. When passing legislation the *Storting* was to divide itself into two parts, the *Odelsting* and the *Lagting*. The rules on suffrage were liberal for their period, as almost half of all men over the age of twenty-five got the vote. This meant that farmers were politically influential s not only as voters, but also as prospective members of Parliament, and no other country could equal Norway on that point. The Eidsvoll Constitution was thus a compromise between absolutism and democracy.

On 17 May 1814 the work on the Constitution was concluded, and the Constitutional Assembly unanimously voted Christian Frederik king in a free, self-governing and independent Norway.

Into a union with Sweden

But danger was not far away. The great powers suspected that Christian Frederik was playing a double game, and trade between Denmark and Norway was cut off by a new blockade. On the

Continent Napoleon had been beaten, and Crown Prince Carl Johan was now free to implement the terms of the Peace of Kiel.

Christian Frederik attempted to get the great powers to recognise an independent Norway, but he was unsuccessful and, at the end of July, Carl Johan attacked southern Norway with a force of 40–50,000 war-hardened troops. Christian Frederik led an army of 30,000 badly trained soldiers and the war was soon over. The Norwegians retreated, and on 14 August the factions made a truce at Moss. Carl Johan accepted the Eidsvoll Constitution as a basis for negotiations, promising that the Swedes would not put forward constitutional amendments other than those necessary to unite Norway and Sweden. He demanded that Christian Frederik should convene an extraordinary meeting of the *Storting*, abdicate from the throne and leave the country.

Carl Johan got his way. He was spared occupying Norway, with all the bitterness that would have entailed. Christian Frederik decreed an election for an extraordinary *Storting* which met in Kristiania on 8 October. Two days later the King abdicated and, on the same afternoon, he left the country. That was the end of Christian Frederik's adventure in Norway, and it was to be twenty-five years before he would be able to call himself King of Denmark.

The *Storting* immediately agreed that Norway should enter into a union with Sweden, and then the negotiations commenced. By and large, the Norwegian negotiators came off well. The new Constitution declared that the Norwegian government had to be split in two, with one part in Kristiania and the other in Stockholm where the King resided, and Norway was not permitted to have an independent foreign policy. But despite Norway clearly being the weaker partner in the union, the King's power had been reduced in comparison with the Eidsvoll Constitution. He could no longer declare war or make peace without the consent of the *Storting*, nor was he allowed to appoint Swedes to official posts in Norway. Norway was also to have its own flag and its own bank, and the revised Constitution's first paragraph stated: "The Kingdom of Norway is a free, self-governing, indivisible and inalienable realm unified with Sweden under one king." Much had been won in the space of ten dramatic months.

The constitutional revisions were finished on 4 November, and the *Storting* elected Carl XIII as King of Norway.

From 1814 to 1905

Crisis and the battle for independence

An economic crisis hit Norway as soon as the Napoleonic Wars were over. Although the blockade had been lifted, it took time for the timber trade with Great Britain to get going again, and the British put heavy tariffs on Norwegian timber to protect imports from Canada. The timber crisis also affected shipping, and the great fire at the Drammen timber yards in 1817 made the situation even more difficult. The vast majority of the old, rich bourgeoisie went bankrupt during these years. First and foremost it was a crisis for the upper classes; as farmers managed to get by with what they produced on their farms and what they could barter, market conditions abroad had less effect on them.

The state, too, lost money in the post-war crisis because export tariffs were a very significant part of national receipts. As if this was not enough, the young nation had an enormous rate of inflation. In the years prior to 1814, King Frederik VI had printed money to finance the wars, as had Christian Frederik in 1814. Carl Johan in Sweden carefully watched developments in Norway. Was the Norwegian state too weak to be allowed to live? In Norway most leading politicians believed that financial probity was a prerequisite to retaining independence.

The Norwegians succeeded, but it was a slow process. In 1816 the *Storting* introduced a monetary unit called the *spesidaler* and set up the Bank of Norway (*Norges Bank*). The national bank had the monopoly on printing notes, and the value of the *spesidaler* was to be secured by a capital stock of precious metal in the bank worth 2–3 million spesidaler. The idea was that people should make voluntary contributions to the stock, but their generosity did not stretch far

The royal palace in Kristiania stands at the end of Carl Johan's street. It was erected by the architect Hans Ditlev Linstow between 1825 and 1848 in the classical style. The painting, from 1882, is the work of Fritz Thaulow.

enough, so the *Storting* raised the "silver tax". People of means had to pay a special tax to the bank, but only in silver, not paper money. Right across the country citizens and farmers had to give their silver heirlooms to the national bank, but the deposits took time to come in, and it was not until 1842 that the Bank of Norway had gathered enough silver to convert the banknotes.

But it was particularly the debt settlement with Denmark that caused tension in the relationship with Sweden. At the Peace of Kiel, Carl Johan and Frederik VI had agreed that Norway should pay its part of the joint Dano-Norwegian national debt, and around 1820 the Danes began to press for what they were owed. However, the *Storting* was unwilling to pay, as Norway had never ratified the Peace of Kiel, and the country was poor. But in this matter Denmark was supported by the great powers of Europe, and Carl Johan, who had become king in 1818, threatened the *Storting*: "If you want to remain independent, pay Denmark its due. If you want unification with Sweden, then *don't* pay!" In May 1821 the King announced that he intended to assemble 6,000 soldiers for a military exercise in Kristiania. The *Storting* now feared a coup and gave in. Norway had to pay.

In the autumn of 1814 Crown Prince Carl Johan had been keen to reach a peaceful settlement with the Norwegians, but shortly after he had assumed the crown he decided the time was ripe for a constitutional revision that would bolster the crown at the expense of the *Storting*. The political climate of Europe was undergoing an anti-democratic reaction, and the King hoped to win support for his Norwegian policy from the great powers. In the autumn of 1821 he proposed several alterations to the Constitution. The King wanted the right to remove all officials apart from judges. The *Storting* was only to assemble every five years, and the King would have the right to dissolve the *Storting* and appoint the presiding officers. Worst of all was the King's demand for an absolute veto in legislative matters. These proposals were put forward several times under threat of military action, but the *Storting* would not back down and threw out all suggestions for change. The representatives viewed the Constitution of 1814 as a bulwark against oppression and an overweening monarchy, and the *Storting*, dominated as it was by officials, did not take kindly to the King's attack on the official classes' position within society. Not even the great powers came to Carl Johan's aid since they wanted a Europe with a balance of power. A relatively independent Norway would not harm this stability, but for Russia a strengthened Swedish monarchy was a direct threat.

Another bone of contention was 17 May, Norway's Constitution Day. Ever since 1814 a number of people had observed the day, but as the 1820s progressed the celebrations became more widespread, something that did not please Carl Johan. He viewed 17 May as a day of revolt and thought it would be better to celebrate the 4 November. The *Storting* tried to dampen the ecstasy over independence so as not to provoke the King, but on 17 May 1829 there were serious clashes in Kristiania. The steamship *Constitutionen* arrived in the city that hot Sunday, and people gathered to cheer. A large crowd assembled at the *Storting*, and the city authorities sent in soldiers to disperse the peaceful throng. Even thought no one was killed, "the Battle of the Market Place" had lasting consequences. The Swedish governor-general in Kristiania, Balthazar von Platen (1766–1829), felt the wrath of the people after this scandalous display of force. He said himself that he was "spat on and reviled from all sides". After this, it was impossible for the King to appoint a Swede as governor-general in Norway, and in the years that followed it became normal to celebrate the 17 May – once again Carl Johan had suffered defeat at the hands of the Norwegians. During the 1830s the controversy died down somewhat, and by the time the King died in 1844 he was actually popular in Norway.

Sweeping changes occurred in Norwegian agriculture during the latter part of the 19th century. Steam threshing machines were a marvellous innovation, and it was common for several farmers to get together to raise the money to buy one. This picture is from Nes in Hedmark.

The Hjula textile factory on the River Aker in Kristiania was founded in 1849. The majority of workers in the textile industry were women. The picture was commissioned by the factory owner in 1887–88 from the painter Wilhelm Peters.

A state of government officials and a parliament of peasants

It is usual to label the Norwegian state in the decades after 1814 a "the officials' state". The officials from the period of absolutism retained their positions of power, and in local communities district governors, tax-collectors, magistrates, clergymen and officers were unchallenged leaders. In addition there were professors from the university, departmental heads at the new ministries and, above all, the King's counsellors. During the first half of the 19th century Norway had about 2,000 civil servants, but though they were few in number, they made up for it with solidarity, class consciousness, nepotism and influence. The Constitution of 1814 was primarily the work of officials, and it was the officials in the *Storting* who had defended it against Carl Johan's attacks in the 1820s, as protecting the Constitution was synonymous with protecting the state bureaucracy. Nor did the constitutional paragraph decreeing that two thirds of the members of the *Storting* should be elected from rural districts curb the officials' influence. The farmers' political alignment was not very strong and they often voted officials into the *Storting*. The fact that Norway lacked an aristocracy and a bourgeoisie that could challenge the official classes socially and politically, merely emphasises the unique position they occupied. In 1821 the *Storting* had, against the King's will, passed legislation that abolished all noble titles and privileges, and it took some time for the upper middle classes to get back on their feet again after the years of crisis.

There was a cultural divide between farmers and officials. Most officials had been educated in Copenhagen; they knew Latin and understood the social niceties. Accordingly, they often looked on farmers as "coarse", even though many had, in the euphoria of independence, praised "the free, Norwegian yeomanry".

From the late 1820s the farmers were on the offensive. Before elections to the *Storting* in 1832 farmers' leaders urged that farmers should elect their own people to the *Storting* – and not officials. And the campaign bore fruit. The *Storting* that assembled in 1833 had a majority of farmers and was later called the "peasant parliament". In the next election, too, the farmers secured a majority.

Two matters were particularly important to the farmers. In the first place they wanted to cut back national expenditure to reduce taxes as much as possible. Many spoke disparagingly of an official class that produced nothing, but simply lived off the sweat of others. The Peasant Parliament cut taxes and increased duty on a number of imports, shifting much of the burden from rural to urban society. The farmers presumably felt that they got little return for investing in the state. For people who lived in a largely self-sufficient econo-

The steam packet *Haakon Adalstein* was built for Det nordenfjeldske Dampskibselskab of Trondheim in 1873. It went down off the west coast of Sweden in 1947.

my, road building and administration was not of much importance, and the military was unpopular because only men from the peasant classes were liable to compulsory military service.

Another major issue was local self-government. In 1833 a group of farmers proposed that each municipality should be governed by a small group of representatives called a local committee *(formannskap)*. The aim was to reduce the influence of officials in the local community. Here, too, the farmers triumphed and the Local Committees Act *(Formannskapsloven)* was passed in 1837. A local board elected by the people was given powers in certain areas, for example, school buildings, teachers' salaries, local roads and care of the poor. On the other hand, the state could place responsibilities on local government, and these grew considerably. To begin with, local elections were poorly supported, but from the middle of the century the interest picked up.

At the 1838 elections the farmers lost their majority. Once again they had elected officials, and a new generation of these now came to dominate both the *Storting* and the government. These new leaders wanted to make the government more active; they believed that material progress was best for the country, and they worked at promoting more liberal industrial legislation.

Towards a new society 1800–1850

In 1800 there were almost 900,000 people in Norway, and the numbers rose sharply during the century. In 1865 the figure was 1.7 million and in 1900 2.2 million. Of particular importance was the drop in infant mortality.

Historians have pointed to several reasons for the increase in population. Nutrition improved because herring and potatoes had replaced barley porridge as the daily fare of ordinary people. Hygiene also got better. As early as the 18th century most houses in the east of the country had got fireplaces with chimneys, or stoves. This made houses cleaner because there was no more soot and smoke from the old hearths which only had a hole in the roof for the smoke. Now the west and north of the country followed suit, and by 1850 fireplaces and stoves were common in most areas. Also of importance was the institution of district medical officers at the end of the 18th century, and in 1801 the authorities introduced smallpox vaccination.

Before 1850 rural society managed to accommodate the growth

in population, and much new land was cleared. This required labour, and the number of smallholders and their families continued to rise until it peaked in about 1850 at 67,000, but by then there was little space left in many rural communities. Farmers had the means to buy better implements, and iron ploughs and harrows gave increased yields. Even so, we cannot at this period speak of a revolution in Norwegian husbandry.

Emigrant Halvor Bøe and family outside their first home at Edmore, North Dakota, about 1900.

The cities expanded at the same time. The capital Kristiania increased its population from 9,000 in about 1800 to almost 40,000 in 1855. From being a sleepy provincial town it was well on the way to becoming a modern metropolis.

The first emigration to America occurred during this period. In 1825 the sloop *Restaurationen* sailed from Stavanger heading for New York with fifty-two passengers, Quaker families who were leaving Norway for religious reasons. The "sloop people" settled in the fertile Fox River Valley in northern Illinois. Gradually Norwegian pioneer settlements were founded in the Mid-West, and the efforts of the forerunners made it easier for others to follow. But mass emigration did not begin until the 1860s and from then until 1930 800,000 Norwegians emigrated to America. Today there are as many people of Norwegian descent in the USA as there are in Norway.

During the 1840s the textile industry grew up in Norway, an

Norway's first railway connected Kristiania with Eidsvoll and was opened in 1854.

entirely new industry and a clear departure from the old mines and sawmills we know from the 18th century. In only a few years textile factories sprang up along the River Aker in Kristiania and near Bergen, some of them with more than a hundred employees. The factory owners bought machinery and equipment from Great Britain, which had rescinded its embargo on the export of machinery in 1843, and from there they also got expertise. The textile factories supplied the home market in this first phase of industrialisation in Norway. But the machines needed servicing, and soon Norwegians would start producing and developing machines themselves. This was the background to the establishment of the first mechanical workshops in the 1840s.

At this time rural society began to feel the effects of population. The competition for jobs stiffened and it became difficult to get a smallholding. In 1848–49 the country was hit by an economic crisis. Mine owners and timber dealers faced sales difficulties which led to lower wages and unemployment for forestry workers, timber carters and charcoal burners. This is the backdrop against which one must view the Thrane Movement that grew up in about 1850.

Over New Year 1848–49, a young student called Marcus Thrane set up the first Workers' Union. Two years later there were 400 Workers' Unions throughout the country with around 30,000 members. It was mainly smallholders, labourers and craftsmen who organised themselves into unions, but also leading cultural figures like the writers Henrik Ibsen (1828–1906) and Aasmund Olavsson Vinje (1818–1870), took part. The Thranites fought for equality, demanding universal franchise for men, universal military service, better primary schools and equality before the law. They also wanted cheaper goods, and the abolition of the corn tax was a major demand. Finally, they called for land to be made more freely available.

Theodor Kittelsen designed this sardine tin label in 1905.

The discontent expressed can be explained by population pressures and lack of land, but Marcus Thrane also took ideas from abroad. He had visited London and Paris and was acquainted with the ideas that had suffused the February Revolution of 1848. Officials and farmers feared the Thranites who spoke of "revolution", and in 1851 the authorities arrested Thrane and other leaders of the movement. Thrane himself was not released from prison until 1858, when he emigrated to America. The movement he had started had died out.

Into the industrial society

It is impossible to understand the rapid development of the second half of the 19th century without taking a look outside Norway's frontiers where the whole of Europe was in flux. Germany and Italy had united into populous states, industrialisation gathered pace and railways linked the entire Continent. This meant a greater demand for goods and services – even from little Norway on the outskirts of Europe – and so, for better or worse, Norwegian industry became more closely linked with countries abroad. Norway got richer, but also more affected by international economic conditions. Most people got the taste for new products, and imports of sugar, chocolate, Mediterranean fruits, coffee and tea increased. Wide swathes of the population switched to the money economy.

During the 1840s and 1850s the *Storting* passed a succession of laws that eased domestic trade. Now, anyone who wanted to could set up as a craftsman, whether in town or village, and a shopkeeper no longer needed to be a burgher. Sawmill privileges were abolished so that anyone could run a sawmill. This sort of trade policy reflected the economic liberalism that held sway in the rest of Europe, and the *Storting* also agreed to abolish many protective tariffs. Trade should be allowed to flow as freely as possible across national frontiers.

Road construction increased, and in the course of fifty years the length of the road network was doubled. Steamships began to operate regular services up and down the coast and on the largest lakes, and in 1854 the country's first railway opened from Kristiania to Eidsvoll. The line principally carried lumber from Øyeren to Kristiania, but also farm produce to a capital that was growing rapidly and required fresh food from the surrounding areas. Three quarters of today's railway system had been completed by 1910. In 1855 the first telegraph line was opened, and soon telegraph wires stretched right across the country. Norway got its first telephone line in 1880, and the inventor, Alexander Graham Bell (1847–1922), was present at the opening. Even mail services improved when the postal rate for the entire country was unified.

Between 1850 and 1880 Norwegian shipping enjoyed its third golden age. The merchant fleet increased its net tonnage from 300,000 to 1.5 million, and the ships got larger. Around 1880, Norwegian ships employed 60,000 seamen, and the country had the third largest mercantile marine in the world after Great Britain and the USA.

There were several reasons why Norwegians did well in this area. Sailing was the obvious method for goods transport, and between 1840 and 1870 world trade increased by more than 50% every decade. Populous Great Britain was Norway's most important trading partner, and the British were dependent on shipped supplies. Furthermore, when the British Navigation Act was rescinded in 1849, ships of any nationality could carry goods to Great Britain, and Norwegian shipowners grasped the opportunity.

A new phase of Norwegian industrialisation began in the 1860s when the country got its first export-oriented industry. Steam engines took over as motive power in the sawmills, planing mills were set up, and in 1863 the country got its first wood pulping factory that manufactured paper. Gradually, the pulp mills began using water turbines which gave the pulping machines greater power. The first Norwegian cellulose factory began operating in 1874. Planing machines and turbines were manufactured in the machine shops, which were expanding rapidly. The canning industry is also worth mentioning in terms of exports.

Between 1850 and 1900 Norwegian fish exports increased manyfold. Parts of the fishing fleet were also modernised, but not without dissent. In 1890–91 the painter Gunnar Berg depicted what was known as the Battle of Trollfjord in Lofoten, in which fishermen in small boats and those in steam trawlers clashed. The former feared that the purse nets might take their livelihoods away. The picture now hangs in the Council Chamber in Svolvær.

This new industry required capital. A large amount came from abroad, especially Great Britain, and foreigners wanted to invest because Norway had natural resources and cheap labour. The Norwegian commercial banks, which were founded around 1850, also gradually managed to access valuable capital. By the turn of the century industry accounted for 28% of gross national product, and over a quarter of all workers were employed in it. People from the country districts streamed into the cities and built-up areas to find work. In 1870 roughly 20% of the population lived in towns and built-up areas. In about 1900 that figure had risen to well over 30%.

Upheavals in agriculture

Around 1850 most farms were self-sufficient, even though it was common everywhere in the country for farmers to take other work as well: forestry, river driving, charcoal burning or fishing. The spinning wheel and loom were in constant use, farmers made their own tools in the farm smithies, and found materials for wooden implements and kitchen utensils in the forests; the women made cheese and butter and distilled spirits. Fifty years later market agriculture had become established in most parts of the country. By this time, new tools had made farms more efficient and the need for small-holders and farm workers was less; thousands of people had there-fore moved to the cities or emigrated to America.

Emigration and exodus had robbed the countryside of labour. And so many farmers were keen to employ labour-saving machines, and some began to start rotating crops and manuring with artificial fertilisers. Good iron ploughs gave higher yields and horse rakes, sowing drills, reapers and threshing machines needed fewer workers.

To make all these changes, farmers needed capital, and the state took the initiative in helping by, for example, founding The Kingdom of Norway's Mortgage Bank (*Kongeriket Norges Hypothek-bank*) in 1851. The bank was a state run lending institution which could attract foreign capital to the country and then make low cost, long-term mortgage loans to rural industries. State run agricultural schools grew up all over the country where farmers could glean knowledge and inspiration, and in 1859 the State Agricultural College (*Landbrukshøyskolen*) at Ås came into existence.

In 1896 some farmers from the east of the country founded the first farmers' pressure group, the Norwegian Farmers' Association (*Norsk Landmannsforbund*).

Even though farmers organised and made demands, few of them considered using the might of the state for their own ends. Instead, they wanted to lower taxes and national expenditure and transfer power to local councils and their executive committees. However, in order to achieve such a decentralisation the farmers and their sup-porters had to win power centrally.

Parliamentary government and political parties

In the 1860s, farmer and *Storting* representative Søren Jaabæk (1814–1894) set up the Society of Farmers' Friends (*Bondevennene*) an organisation that attracted around 25,000 members. This, the first electoral association in Norway, which covered the whole coun-try apart from Finnmark, helped to elect more farmers to the *Storting*, and by 1868 they were in the majority. The Farmers' Friends wanted local government strengthened. They did not like the government using money to assist the new industries, and many felt that the tax burden fell disproportionately upon farmers. But the

The philologist and writer Ivar Aasen (1813–1896) created *Landsmål*, a new written language based on the Norwegian dialects. In 1885 the *Storting* terrified a lot of people by deciding to give it equal status with the official written language, *Riksmål*. Olaf Gulbransson called this drawing from 1898 "The language ogres advance on Kristiania". In the background is Ivar Aasen leading his literary colleagues Arne Garborg and Per Sivle.

Farmers' Friends were a loosely linked organisation and the society died out in the 1870s.

What was required to weaken the civil servants' state was firm leadership from the top. And this came about when Søren Jaabæk and his supporters in the *Storting* formed an alliance with the lawyer and *Storting* representative Johan Sverdrup (1816–1892), who was the leader of a group of radical academics. Sverdrup had first been elected to the *Storting* in 1851, and during the constitutional battle of the 1870s and 1880s he stood out as one of the great political leaders in Norwegian history.

The government was the *Storting* opposition's most implacable adversary. At this time officials still dominated politics, and the King appointed only civil servants to cabinet posts. But the *Storting* strengthened its position in 1869 when annual *Storting* sessions were voted in, and now it was possible for Sverdrup and his followers to conduct a coherent oppositional campaign. The struggle for power could begin in earnest.

In 1872 the *Storting* discussed a suggested constitutional amendment to the effect that cabinet ministers had a duty to attend *Storting* sessions to defend the policies they were implementing, as Sverdrup reasoned: "(...) at this moment, just as all power and might is gathering here in this hall to decide the highest and most important social affairs, a great awakening is going through our land (...)" The result was that the *Storting* passed the constitutional amendment, enabling cabinet ministers to be "rooted out of the gloom of their offices".

But the King refused to approve the resolution and pointed to the division of powers upon which the Constitution was built. In addition, he and the government maintained that the King had an absolute veto in constitutional matters, although not a word of this appeared in the Constitution. Sverdrup and the farmers in turn claimed that the King had no right of veto in constitutional matters, and the amendment was passed by three further *Storting*s. The government, however, consistently advised the King to withhold his assent.

The farmers' opposition in the *Storting* decided to opt for the weapon of last resort: to impeach the government before the Court of Impeachment. The Court of Impeachment is a special court in which representatives of the *Lagting* sit together with the Supreme Court Judges, while the *Odelsting* presses charges. In the elections of 1882, Sverdrup's supporters, by that time usually called Liberal (*Venstre*), won 83 out of 114 seats. Several cabinet ministers, including Prime

Minister Christian August Selmer (1816–1889), were sentenced to lose their positions, while others were fined. By a majority, the Court of Impeachment ruled that the government should not have advised the King to withhold his assent in the "cabinet ministers" affair.

In utmost secrecy King Oscar II planned a coup d'etat, but his plans were mothballed, and in June 1884 he asked the leader of the majority party in the *Storting*, Johan Sverdrup, to form a government. For the first time a politician had been put in charge of the government because he had a majority of *Storting* representatives behind him. The civil servants' state had suffered a defeat and parliamentary government had come to Norway.

The "cabinet ministers" affair and the battle over the King's right to veto led to the creation of the Liberal Party and the Conservatives (*Høyre*). The Liberal Party was supported by the farmers, but teachers and petty officials also voted for the party, and in the 1880s it dealt

The writer Bjørnstjerne Bjørnson and the composer Edvard Grieg in the garden of Grieg's home, "Trollhaugen" near Bergen. Grieg is indisputably Norway's greatest composer, and his music contains many elements of Norwegian folk music. In his day, Bjørnson was the Norwegian with the greatest reputation abroad and he wrote Norway's national anthem *Ja, vi elsker dette landet*. He was awarded the Nobel Prize for Literature in 1903.

Norway's most renowned artist, Edvard Munch, painted Norway's most famous writer, Henrik Ibsen, at the legendary Grand Café in Kristiania. The picture was painted between 1906–10.

with many important issues. A new law on franchise gave the vote to about half of all men, but it was not until 1898 that universal suffrage for men came in. The two main written languages *landsmål* and *riksmål* were given equal status, so that Norway now had two official variations. A Jury Law decreed that a jury of laymen should determine guilt in criminal cases, and the Education Acts of 1889 made seven years of schooling compulsory for all children. But Sverdrup ran into problems. When the government proposed a writer's pension for the social critic Alexander Kielland (1849–1906), the Liberal Party split. The Conservatives, who were supported by officials and the bourgeoisie, took over the government in 1889.

But people were organising outside the *Storting* as well. In the 1880s and 1890s it became more common for male and female workers to organise themselves into trade unions and national professional associations, and in 1899 these associations merged into the Norwegian Federation of Trade Unions (*Arbeidernes Faglige Landsorganisasjon, "LO"*). A year later the employers started the

Norwegian Employers' Confederation (*Norsk Arbeidsgiverforening*) to meet the growing threat of organised labour. In 1887 the *Det Norske Arbeiderparti* (The Norwegian Labour Party) was started. The party quickly turned to socialism and demanded shorter working time and the vote for all women and men. In 1903 it got four *Storting* representatives, three from the fishing county of Troms. It seems that not just industrial workers, but country people too, were interested in voting for socialism.

Social development created new opportunities, especially for middle-class women. Women gained the right to attend middle and secondary schools, and primary schools, the post office and telegraph services all required qualified staff. In 1884 women were permitted to sit all the degree exams at the University. A number of leading male figures took up the women's issue in social debate, and the plays of Henrik Ibsen and Bjørnstjerne Bjørnson aroused controversy. The Norwegian Women's Rights League (*Norsk Kvinnesaksforbund*), which had been founded in 1884, had both male and female members. Women set up the Norwegian Women's Suffrage Association (*Norsk Kvinnestemmerettsforening*) the following year, but their demands met with opposition both from within the *Storting* and outside it. Many people maintained that women should work in the home, that they were unstable and unsuited to positions of responsibility. Still, women penetrated one bastion after another. At first it was only women with a certain income who were eligible to vote, but in 1913 the *Storting* gave all women the vote. The first permanent female *Storting* representative took her seat in 1924.

Dissolution of the union in 1905

Ever since 1814 Norway had been the "junior partner" in the union, and towards the end of the 19th century the union conflict flared up again. Many people felt that the union was of less and less economic importance to Norway. The best example of this was the way the Swedes had abolished the free trade agreement between the two countries – *Mellomriksloven* – in 1897. Swedish foreign policy also alarmed Norwegians who felt a close affinity with Great Britain. In the 1880s King Oscar II stated that "Germany is, and should be, our closest and most natural ally". Norwegians were particularly unhappy about having a Swedish foreign minister, and that both countries shared consulates abroad. Only consuls exclusively representing

Norway could look after the interests of Norwegian economic life.

This is not to say that it was simply finances and Norwegian inferiority complexes that wore away at the union. The concept of the nation state – one people one state – had gained acceptance in Europe, and Norway embarked on a process of nation building that emphasised the characteristic elements of the country's history and culture. Furthermore, many Norwegians felt that the union acted as a brake on democratisation. Norway was the first country in Europe to institute parliamentary government (1884) and universal suffrage for men (1889).

During the 1890s the Liberal Party took the lead in trying to solve the foreign representation problem. The party took the line that Norway should have its own foreign minister. At the very least, the country should be given its own consular service at the earliest opportunity. The Conservatives supported the latter demand, but insisted that a new arrangement could only be effected after negotiations with Sweden. In 1895, the Liberals were forced to accept the negotiated route as the Swedes were threatening war. In the years

Norwegian soldiers sharpen their sabres during the break-up of the union in 1905. The picture was taken at Gardermoen.

Opposite page:
At the turn of the 20th century, the biologist, polar explorer and politician Fridtjof Nansen (1861–1930) was one of Norway's best known and most respected men. He had crossed Greenland on skis in 1889, nearly reached the North Pole in 1895 and was the government's envoy during the dissolution of the union in 1905. This picture was taken in a Kristiania studio.

King Haakon VII carrying Crown Prince Olav is welcomed by Prime Minister Christian Michelsen in 1905.

that followed, the two parties alternated in government and in the end the negotiations were shelved. During this period the *Storting* voted more money to defence, and in southern Norway, along the border with Sweden, fortifications were being built. These were obstructive forts, earth mounds with reinforced command chambers and connecting passages. Norway ordered four new armoured ships from Great Britain, as well as 140 fast firing German guns.

A Swedish initiative brought new negotiations on the Consular Service in 1902. The parties agreed that Norway should get her own consuls, and that the Swedes should draw up a bill for the legislation. This agreement split the Liberal Party yet again. Radicals within the party believed that such an agreement might prevent Norway getting its own foreign service. Moderates within the party, led by shipowner and Storting representative Christian Michelsen (1857–1925), broke away and went to the electorate with the Conservatives calling themselves the Coalition Party (*Samlings-*

partiet). The author Bjørnstjerne Bjørnson gave the party its slogan: "Negotiation is the only way we know!"

The Coalition Party won the election, and after it came the Swedish Consulate Bill. Norway would get her own consuls, but the foreign minister would continue to be Swedish, and the Norwegian consuls would answer to him. The Norwegians could not agree to this, and the parties prepared for battle under the slogan "Out of the union!" Christian Michelsen became prime minister of a broad coalition government in which everyone except Labour (*Arbeiderpartiet*) was included.

In the spring of 1905 the *Storting* passed an act establishing a separate Norwegian consular service. When the King refused to give his assent, the government resigned. On 7 June the *Storting* unanimously voted "that the union with Sweden under one king is suspended because the King has ceased to function as the Norwegian King". Their most important argument was that he had failed to procure a new government for the country.

The 7 June vote caused consternation in Sweden, and conservative forces called for war. Norwegian soldiers were ordered to defend its borders, but fortunately moderate forces prevailed in Sweden, and new negotiations took place. The *Storting* tried to placate the Swedes. It offered the crown of Norway to a prince from the Swedish royal family, but the offer was refused. In August there was a plebiscite on the union. Only 184 men were for the continuation of the union, and the women collected 250,000 signatures supporting dissolution. After a tough round of negotiations that autumn, Norway agreed to destroy the majority of the border forts. The threat of war was over.

There was one problem remaining: should Norway continue to be a monarchy? A great many Norwegian politicians were republicans, but for tactical reasons they moderated their opinions to soothe the great European monarchies. As a result the Norwegian government the Danish Prince, Carl, to become the Norwegian King. He was married to Princess Maud, daughter of the British King, and they had a two-year-old son. The Prince insisted that the people should be asked their opinion in a plebiscite, and 80% voted for monarchy.

One snowy November day in 1905 the new royal family came ashore in Kristiania. The King took the name Haakon VII and called his son Olav. After centuries of union, Norway could at last take her place amongst the autonomous nations of Europe.

Norway the free

1905–1940

The new working day

After the breakup of the union politicians spoke of the dawning of "a new working day" in Norway. Water power gave the country an advantage, and in the years immediately after 1905 industry had its great breakthrough, and became economically important. The cities continued to grow, and farmers got bigger markets and better prices, so that the changes in agricultural society got ever faster. Communications, too, continued to expand; water power made it possible to provide more houses with electric power, and in the biggest cities electric trams began running. The first motor ships presaged a revolution in the fishing and merchant fleets and, simultaneously, the first cars began to travel on Norwegian roads.

The union battle with Sweden had brought politicians together, but after 1905 normal life returned. The Coalition Party fell apart when Christian Michelsen stepped down as prime minister in 1907, and the Liberals and the Conservatives rebuilt their party organisations. However, Michelsen's ideas lived on in the Liberal Left (*Det frisinnede venstre*) which was founded in 1909, and the party co-operated closely with the Conservatives. It was these non-socialist parties that jockeyed with the Labour Party for the voters' favour in the decade prior to the First World War.

Around the turn of the century foreign and Norwegian capitalists began buying up waterfalls at an enormous rate. Farmers who owned waterfalls were willing to sell because they needed the money to run their farms, or to emigrate to America, and the offers were sometimes woefully small. In 1906 foreigners owned three quarters

Theodor Kittelsen's painting of this power station at Rjukan speaks of how man has managed to tame the forces of nature and expresses the intense trust in technological advance that characterised the early years of the 20th century.

of all developed waterfalls, and this led to the fear that national independence was threatened. Who should own the waterfalls, mines and forests of Norway?

Many people thought that the state ought to place restrictions on the owners. The people living around an industrial concern should get cheap electricity, and its workers should be well housed. The state should secure taxes from the developers who also ought to use Norwegian goods and services. Such radical views caused debate in the *Storting*, but the result was that both Norwegian and foreign companies had to get permission (a concession) before they could begin a project. This bartering tool made it possible for the state to set conditions, and the law stated that waterfalls with dams were to revert to the state after sixty to eighty years. Foreigners were not allowed to purchase forest at all. The concession laws may have slowed the pace of Norwegian industry, but society ensured its control over natural resources.

Industrialisation did not provide affluence for everyone. Many people in cities felt insecure because the old interdependence of the rural community was lacking, and unemployment, alcoholism, prostitution and housing shortage were very apparent in the working-class districts. Fairer distribution was a key demand of the Labour Party and the unions, but also of non-socialists. There were many, in the Liberal Party particularly, who thought that the state had a duty to protect the poorest and improve the lot of working people. Accordingly, the *Storting* passed a series of reforms in the period leading up to the First World War. Sick pay, factory inspection, worker protection laws and the ten hour day are examples of this. In addition, children born out of wedlock had their rights assured.

Norway during the First World War

In 1905 the *Storting* and the government wanted to keep the country out of international conflicts, and they followed the example of Denmark and Sweden and adopted a policy of neutrality. However, when the First World War broke out in the summer of 1914, Norway position became difficult. Despite her neutrality, a great many of her people sympathised with Britain, and the Norwegian economy depended on a good relationship with the British. Great Britain provided important goods like oil and coal, and the merchant fleet had to avoid a British blockade at all costs. The British knew how to

The Norwegian merchant-man *Consul Persson* was sunk during the First World War.

exploit the situation. In 1915, for example, they forced Norway to halt most of her fish exports to Germany, while her mercantile marine gave Great Britain and her Allies valuable support. For this reason Norway has been called "the neutral ally".

This policy resulted in a tense relationship with Germany, and German U-boats severely harried the Norwegian merchant fleet. Half the fleet was sunk, and more than 2,000 seamen lost their lives.

There were several reasons why Norway was not directly drawn into the war. Neither the Triple Alliance, headed by Germany, or the entente between Great Britain, France and Russia wanted to draw the country in. Both blocs benefited from Norwegian neutrality, and because Norway's military power was relatively small, it could actually have been quite risky to have her as an ally. Nobody wanted to tie up troops on Norwegian soil.

For some Norwegians the two first years of war were years of huge profits. Share prices rose as the demand for Norwegian goods and services increased, and a few amassed huge wealth through speculation, but subsequently most of these "noveaux riches" went bankrupt.

The final two years of the war brought harder times for most. The authorities wanted to mitigate the effects of high prices, but measures only came at the eleventh hour. Each district got its Supplies Committee to control the national distribution of food. Sugar and corn monopolies were introduced, and it became illegal to use potatoes and corn for distilling spirits. In 1916 the authorities banned the import of spirits, and the following year this was extended to fortified wines. In the last year of the war corn, flour, sugar, bread, coffee and tea were rationed, and every family got a ration card.

High prices, black market trading and the frittering away of money by the newly rich irritated ordinary people, and the war years exacerbated the class divisions in Norway.

The economy and industry during the inter-war years

A typical characteristic of economic development in the years between the First and Second World Wars, was lack of stability. After a brief upturn from 1918 to 1920, Norway was hit by falling prices and marketing problems, and throughout the 1920s both prices and monetary value fluctuated. This caused a battle over wages. The workers used strikes as a weapon, and the employers responded with lock-outs.

The monetary policy of the Bank of Norway during the 1920s reinforced the problems. The bank had issued far too much paper money during the war, and this caused serious inflation and a falling rate of exchange on the krone when peace came. To rectify these problems the Bank of Norway adopted measures to strengthen the krone relative to the pound sterling and the value of gold. The bank reduced the amount of money in circulation and put up the interest rate, but it was not until 1928 that the value of the krone had reached the level the central bank was aiming for.

The increasing value of the krone caused fresh problems. As it became more difficult to get loans and more expensive to have debt, investment in industry declined, and of course people who already had debt were squeezed, as they had to pay interest and make repayments with kroner that were more expensive than when their loans had been advanced.

Many farmers tried to solve their debt crises by producing more. This, coupled with the fact that people in cities had less money to spend on food, meant there was a surplus of agricultural products.

Knut Hamsun (1859–1952) is one of Norway's best known writers. He was awarded the Nobel Prize for Literature in 1920 for his novel "The Growth of the Soil", which is pervaded by a deep scepticism of industrial society. Hamsun's reputation was severely dented during the Second World War when he sided with the Nazis.

The competition between farmers grew tougher, and prices fell. In collaboration with the state, farmers set up marketing boards. These agencies were empowered to regulate the sale of agricultural products. The milk marketing boards, for example, decided how much milk should go for consumption and how much for the production of cheese and butter. The marketing boards set prices, looked after exports and were able to impose taxes on products. The money raised by these taxes was used to keep prices stable.

Fishermen were particularly badly hit by the inter-war crisis. They, too, had borrowed money for new equipment in the boom years after 1905. When export prices fell and servicing loans got more expensive during the 1920s, many fishing families ended up in dire straits. In the most northerly counties, roughly half of all adult men had fishing as their main or subsidiary income. Many of them now no longer had the money to keep a motor boat with a deck and fishing gear, instead they had to fish with handlines from open boats. Incomes fell drastically and in several coastal communities both adults and children struggled against under- and malnourishment.

The crisis in the fishing industry galvanised the politicians. The National Fishery Bank of Norway (*Statens Fiskarbank*), which made generous loans, was founded in 1919. The state also encouraged fishermen to organise. The Norwegian Fishermen's Union (*Norges Fiskarlag*) was set up in 1926, and from the end of the 1920s the *Storting* passed several laws regulating the sale of various fish species. The aim was the same as that of the marketing boards in farming: they would discourage overproduction and hold prices up.

Industrial concerns also tried to work their way out of the crisis by co-operating with companies in the same sector. They agreed common prices, divided up markets or set production quotas. Such cartels were encouraged by the state. The new trust law of 1926 enabled the Trust Control to manage the competitive terms in industry and gave it an ability to regulate the market.

The world economic crisis that began in the USA in 1929 reached Norway the following year. Recent research has put the unemployment rate for 1931 to 1933 at about 10%, and when we look at the 1930s as a whole, up to a tenth of the population was dependent on poor relief. But compared with other countries there was not an especially large number of unemployed in Norway during the inter-war years, apart from the end of the 1920s, when the Bank of Norway's monetary policy led to relatively high joblessness.

It was not only the economic crisis that led to an excess of labour during the 1930s. The generations of young people reaching working age in that decade were larger than previous ones, and the USA had closed its borders to mass immigration. Also, more women were putting off marriage, and many of them were looking for work.

When the price of goods fell and the wage and debt servicing bills got too high, many concerns went bankrupt. This led to the banks losing large amounts of money in unrecovered debts. People began to fear they might lose their savings and rushed to the banks to take out their money. The state pumped considerable sums into the banks, but to little effect. Several banks went bust, and their depositors' money was lost.

Local councils were not immune, either. Unemployment and industrial problems lowered tax receipts, while at the same time outgoings for poor relief and relief work increased. At worst, local councils had to surrender their local autonomy and allow the state to take

A whale being flensed at Grytviken, South Georgia. The whaling station was founded in 1905, but lost much of its importance in the mid-1920s when whale factory ships began to be used in the hunting grounds of the Southern Ocean.

control of their finances. Several of them got loans from the Municipal Bank of Norway (*Norges Kommunalbank*), which had been set up by the *Storting* in 1927.

Such government measures are good examples of the way that the non-socialist majority in the *Storting* was not paralysed by these economic problems. Public responsibility and control increased between 1918 and 1935, and election promises of huge cuts in state costs were never realised.

The inter-war years were not just ones of crisis. Statistics show that the gross national product doubled, and that industrial production rose by about 80%. Even so, there were no more industrial jobs in 1939 than there had been in 1915. One significant cause was that companies began to use new machinery powered by electric motors and to rationalise along American lines.

Those who were fortunate enough to keep their jobs in industry or the public sector, got more for their wages than previously. They bought themselves electric stoves, irons and hot water tanks, and adorned their homes with new furniture, toilets and wash basins. Many also had the money to buy radios, and the most affluent of all purchased private cars. People spent more money on clothes, bicycles and sporting equipment for their spare time. It became common to visit the cinema, listen to the radio, read magazines, smoke cigarettes and eat chocolate.

The majority of the consumer goods that found their way on to the market between the wars was produced by small, newly founded companies often located in the provinces. Many had been started by unemployed people because they could not find other work. They benefited from the fact that Norway, like most other countries, increased tariffs to protect its own industries, and the authorities together with industry produced advertising campaigns encouraging people to buy Norwegian. Both export and import values fell as a proportion of the national product during the inter-war years.

Although many ships had to be laid up in the worst years of crisis, the inter-war period was a time of growth for shipping. In the 1930s only Great Britain and the USA were larger maritime nations than Norway. Norwegian shipowners led the field when it came to replacing steam propulsion with motors, and by 1939 the country had the world's most modern merchant fleet with many specialised ships such as tankers and refrigerator ships.

Non-socialist policy between the wars

During the entire inter-war period, the non-socialist parties got electoral majorities, but were unable to form stable governments. From 1918 to 1935, Norway had nine different governments which, on average, held power for just eighteen months each. Almost all were minority governments, and most of them were based around the Liberal Party.

Even though the workers' movement was growing more powerful and parts of it were talking about revolution and class warfare, the Liberals did not want to be part of a broad anti-socialist bloc. The party wanted to remain above class differences and to use the state to help the weak. The Liberal Party believed that social reforms, price controls and legislation restricting international big business would remove many of the grounds for unhappiness in the working-classes.

The Liberal Party had its power base in the south and west of the country, in areas where people supported New Norwegian (the dialect based written language earlier called *landsmål*; the alternative to the Dano-Norwegian *riksmål*, now called "Book Language"), teetotalism and the Christian lay movement. The party was also keen to lower duties on agricultural products so that food could be brought down in price. This policy led to conflict with the farmers. In 1920 they formed their own party, the Agrarian Party (*Bondepartiet*), which together with Labour made inroads into the Liberal Party's electoral support. In 1936 the Liberals had a 15.9% share of the vote. The party had fallen back by about 4% since 1921.

Until the beginning of the 1930s the Agrarian Party believed that Liberals were over-tolerant of the workers' movement, too keen on state interference in industry and too little concerned with keeping the national and municipal budgets under control. It was, however, necessary that the state should support farming with money for clearance work and corn growing, so that the country could become as self-sufficient as possible and freehold farmers get a better livelihood. The party was convinced that a strong farming community was the best bulwark against the revolutionary socialists.

The elections just after the First World War were very good ones for the Conservatives. The party was concerned about revolutionary undercurrents and proposed several social reforms such as old age pensions and regulated domestic rents, but once the workers' movement became weakened by splits, the Conservatives adopted a more conventional line.

In the 1930s the Conservatives were more obviously the party of industry, with a solid hold on the urban bourgeoisie, especially in the east of the country. Although the Conservatives lost voters, the party managed to retain its position as the largest non-socialist party at every election during the inter-war period. Of the non-socialist representatives, those from the Conservatives were the ones who looked on with greatest dismay as the state's roles and expenditure increased. They maintained that at times of crisis taxes and public expenditure should be reduced as far as possible, to encourage industry to take new initiatives. The Conservatives were sceptical of New Norwegian but had a liberal attitude in matters of religion, alcohol and morality.

As a consequence of widespread strikes and revolutionary threats from the workers' movement, the *Storting* passed several pieces of legislation aimed at protecting civil society. Prison sentences were introduced for those who prevented "blacklegs" from working. A similar fate awaited those who supported unlawful strikes, refused to do military service or agitated against the armed forces. Several of the Labour Party's leaders were imprisoned for anti-military activities.

Nor were Conservative governments averse to calling out the police and army to protect strike-breakers, but these confrontations did not lead to much bloodshed. Over the period 1900–1939 only one person was killed during industrial disputes. Large employers' organisations like the Norwegian Bankers' Association, the Federation of Norwegian Industry and the Farmers' Union helped by building up "Norway's Community Aid" (*Norges Samfunnshjelp*), which supplied industry with alternative labour during industrial disputes. There was also a secret defence corps in the army composed of "dependable" personnel. The political authorities also sanctioned a civil defence force that was trained by army officers. This civil defence force had about 10,000 members.

The greatest anti-socialistic organisation was The Patriotic Union (*Fedrelandslaget*) which was founded in 1925. The union advocated doing battle with the revolutionary workers' movement and promoted non-socialist unity, retrenchment and the cherishing of national values. At its peak the organisation had more than 100,000 members and was supported by well-known figures like Christian Michelsen, Roald Amundsen and Fridtjof Nansen. The Patriotic Union deserved part of the credit for the Conservatives' election win of 1930, but during the 1930s the organisation lost much support, and its rump developed clear fascist tendencies.

Norway also had its offshoot of European fascism. The National Unity Party (*Nasjonal Samling* – "*NS*") was founded in 1933 with Vidkun Quisling as leader. The party took its inspiration from Mussolini's Italy, German Nazism and the Finnish Lappo-movement. The National Unity Party found sympathy amongst those who were disillusioned with non-socialist democracy and who wanted to take up the fight against the workers' movement. The party exploited some of the frustration that grew up during the worst years of crisis.

In elections during the 1930s the National Unity Party achieved only a couple of per cent of the vote and no representatives in the *Storting*. Also wracked by internal dissent and membership decline, by 1939 the National Unity Party had been reduced to a small, isolated sect. No one could then have foreseen that the following year it would get its historic opportunity with the help of German bayonets.

Schism and unification within the workers' movement

Towards the end of the First World War a revolutionary wing took control of the Labour Party. This wing had lost much of its belief that workers' conditions could be improved within existing society. Negotiations with the employers and participation in parliamentary activity was no longer sufficient. A resolution from March 1918 stated that the party had become a "party of revolutionary class struggle" with the right to use "revolutionary mass action in the struggle for the economic liberation of the working classes".

The radicalisation of the workers' movement must be seen in the light of greatly worsened conditions for the great majority of people. In 1917 prices shot right up, while shortages, black market trading and speculation became everyday occurrences. Newly rich stockbrokers wallowed in luxury, while many others had to fight for their daily bread. In the autumn news arrived from Russia that the Bolsheviks had crushed the Tsar's regime and set up a new workers' state. In many places workers' and soldiers' councils were set up along Soviet lines, and in the spring of 1918 the revolutionary faction secured a majority at the Labour Party's conference. The Norwegian Labour Party was the only European social democratic party to vote to join the Communist International, Komintern, which had its headquarters in Moscow.

It did not take long for tensions to mount up between the Labour Party and Komintern. There was growing disquiet in Norway that

This fresco in Oslo City Hall, painted by Reidar Aulie, shows how the Norwegian workers' movement changed its message from one of revolutionary class struggle to social democratic concensus politics focussing on social reforms.

the Soviet Communists demanded that all affiliated parties should blindly follow Moscow's orders. In 1921 the Labour Party's right wing broke away and formed a new social democratic party, and two years later a majority in the Labour Party voted to break with the Communist International. The minority formed itself into the Norwegian Communist Party (*Norges Kommunistiske Parti*) which was accepted as a new member of Komintern. Throughout the 1920s the Norwegian Communist Party lost members and voters to the Labour Party, and by the 1930s the Communists were not even able to send a representative to the *Storting*.

The frustration of the workers' movement at middle-class society increased during the 1920s. This was clearly shown in the Labour Party's battle against 17 May celebrations, the Norwegian flag and the national anthem. As an alternative, the party celebrated 1 May, ran up the red flag and sang the "International". Although the Labour Party had broken with Komintern, many within it had great sympathy for the Soviet Union throughout the inter-war years. Many communities built special centres, "Houses of the People", that became the focus for the workers' movement's political and cultural activities. They were used for party and union meetings, theatre groups, choirs, bands and athletics clubs, which developed a distinct workers' culture.

The bitter tussle between the Labour Party, the Norwegian Social Deomocratic Labour Party (*Sosialdemokratene*) and the Norwegian Communist Party sapped the workers' movement of strength, and the membership of the Norwegian Federation of Trade Unions fell sharply. So it is hardly surprising that the union movement itself wanted an end to the party split. Their efforts paid off. In 1927 the Labour Party and the Social Democratic Labour Party amalgamated and went to the hustings on a platform that stressed old social democratic values. The party now aimed at winning over people with peaceful reforms passed in democratically elected chambers. The election was a success. The Labour Party took over the position as the country's largest party. The non-socialist parties still had a majority in the *Storting*, though negotiations between them to form a government got bogged down. To everyone's surprise, King Haakon stepped in and gave the government to the republican Labour Party, which annually voted against granting money to the royal household.

The country's first labour government took over in January 1928. It laid out a highly provocative manifesto in which it wanted to "prepare for a transition to a socialist social order". Company owners and bankers immediately transferred large amounts of money abroad, and after only fourteen days the government fell. The non-socialist

After the First World War, Fridtjof Nansen did an enormous amount of work for prisoners of war and refugees from Russia and south-east Europe. He was rewarded with the Nobel Peace Prize in 1923. This picture was taken during a visit to Armenia in 1925. Behind Nansen (in a light suit) can be glimpsed one of his close colleagues, Vidkun Quisling.

parties had rapidly reached agreement about a new government once economic stability had been threatened.

These events led to the radical elements in the Labour Party strengthening their position. At their conference in 1930 the party adopted a manifesto which once again included much of the old revolutionary rhetoric. The manifesto caused anxiety amongst non-socialists, who began a powerful counter-offensive prior to elections in the same year. During electioneering they stressed their defence of national, Christian values against the atheism and class politics of the Labour Party. This message really got through, particularly to women, and the election was a defeat for the Labour Party.

The poor election result caused the revolutionary elements within the party to lose support. But unemployment and the social crisis also helped bring the party back to a more moderate line. More and more people were insisting that the party work out new policies to get the country back on its feet again.

In 1933 the Labour Party launched a crisis programme under the slogan "the whole nation at work!". Several of its proposals built on the ideas of the British social economist John Maynard Keynes and lessons drawn from the Soviet planned economy. The manifesto broke with the well established principle that the state should save money during recessions. The idea now was that the state should take out large loans for initiatives that could reduce unemployment. In a "three-year plan for Norway" from the autumn of 1933, the Labour Party suggested that the state should invest large amounts in land clearance, industrial development, power stations, roads and railways. The means of production would not be nationalised, but the state needed better ways of regulating and controlling the economy.

These new crisis policies were the main reason for the Labour Party's huge victory at the polls in the election of 1933. The fascist advance in other parts of Europe made the party even more tractable towards bourgeoisie democracy. This was clearly demonstrated in 1935 when the Norwegian Federation of Trade Unions and the Norwegian Employers' Confederation negotiated a basic agreement for industry which established rules for wage negotiations and wage agreements and enshrined the right of workers to form trade unions and elect shop stewards.

After the election of 1933 there was increasing disquiet in the Agrarian Party as a result of forced sales and unemployment in country districts. The party made several proposals for the state to increase investment in farming, but the Liberal government would not agree. This paved the way for a rapprochement between the Agrarian and Labour parties. In 1935 they agreed on a crisis settlement: the Labour Party would form a government with a promise to increase investment in the rural economy.

The Labour Party government under Johan Nygaardsvold's premiership remained in office until 1945. In the years before the war it espoused moderate reform policies which turned the Labour Party into an accepted partner in parliamentary democracy. The Labour Party was now more concerned with increasing production and social welfare than with class struggle, and the party joined in the 17 May celebrations and all the national values associated with them.

The government fostered optimism and a good, co-operative atmosphere in politics and industry. It also reaped the benefits of better international trading conditions, which caused a greater demand for Norwegian goods.

Norwegian sovereignty over Spitzbergen was regulated by the Spitzbergen Treaty of 1925. The islands were demilitarised and opened up for commercial enterprise to all the signatory states. In 1926, Ny-Ålesund was used as a base for an expedition to the North Pole using the airship *Norge*. Those aboard included the polar researchers Roald Amundsen, Lincoln Ellsworth and Umberto Nobile.

The non-socialist majority in the *Storting* repudiated large national debt and deficit budgets to get the economy going. However, the Labour Party got support from the Agrarian and Liberal parties to raise taxes and duties. This allowed more money to be used for employment and social reforms. The government passed a new Employment Protection Act that gave all employees an eight hour day and nine days holiday. Furthermore, sickness benefit was widened to include new groups of workers, and the old age pension and unemployment benefit were introduced. These reforms increased the state's area of responsibility. At the same time, national cohesion was strengthened.

Foreign and defence policy

At the end of the First World War, the victorious powers came together to found an international organisation that would ensure peace. The League of Nations' pact required member countries to institute sanctions against those who went to war. Once Norway had decided to join, it meant that the country could be forced to take sides if conflicts arose between the great powers.

At the start of the 1920s Norway was involved with the humanitarian work of the League of Nations. As High Commissioner for

Refugees Fridtjof Nansen made a great contribution in Russia, Greece and Turkey, and he led the relief work during the famine in the Ukraine in 1921. The following year he was awarded the Nobel Peace Prize.

Norway was an active participant in disarmament work and wished to be seen as a model for international co-operation. Arbitration agreements were signed with the other Scandinavian countries and a few other states. These obliged the parties to resolve conflict by means of negotiation, mediation and arbitration. But because most of the great powers were hostile, such agreements were of little value.

When the international situation worsened in the latter part of the 1930s, Norway and the other Scandinavian countries announced that they no longer felt themselves constrained to participate in the League of Nations' sanctions. Once again the country put its trust in the old policy of neutrality.

In common with many other European countries, Norway tried to gain control of new territory during the inter-war years. Because Norwegians had a long history of sealing, whaling and exploration in polar regions, it was natural that their attention was focused on such areas. During the peace negotiations after the First World War, Norway wanted control of Spitzbergen. A treaty was made that ensured Norway's sovereignty over the islands, but every country that signed it had the same right to economic activity there. At the end of the 1920s Norway also took control of Jan Mayen, Bouvet Island and Peter I Island. The latter two were of particular interest for whaling in the Antarctic Ocean. Norway also laid claim to large areas of continental Antarctica. In 1939 Dronning Maud's Land was made part of the Norwegian hegemony.

Despite the increase in international tension during the years that followed, defence was not built up according to plan. The belief that Norway would manage to keep out of new wars was strong; the country had been at peace since 1814 and had successfully depended on negotiations when war threatened. Many people thought that the peaceful conclusion of the union conflict with Sweden was the result of skilful diplomacy on the Norwegian part. Few emphasised the fact that rearmament and mobilisation prior to 1905 had strengthened the Norwegian negotiating position. Most, too, were convinced that it was the government's wise foreign policy – and not military might – that had prevented the country from being drawn into the First World War.

The possibility that other countries might want to gain a foothold in Norway was viewed as small. Great Britain was seen as the country that might have the biggest interest in controlling Norwegian territory in a crisis, but this by no means conferred enemy status on the British; on the contrary, it was a generally held view that the British navy would prevent attacks from other powers. If Norway, against all expectation, were forced to chose sides in another major war, most of her citizens were inclined to support the British.

Most politicians were convinced that Norway would not be in a position to repulse an attack from one of the great powers, no matter how much the country prepared. They believed that a powerful military would only have a provocative effect and they did not want to risk large material or human losses. The economic crisis also made it hard to increase the defence budget. Nor did defence planning assume that Norwegian forces would become involved in long-term hostilities. Their main objective was to make it clear that Norway was opposed to any invasion.

When the Labour Party took governmental control in 1935 many feared that they would stick to their anti-militaristic policies. But this did not happen. The party followed the defence policy adopted by the Liberal Party and adhered to the main principles of the defence strategy of the early 1930s. In the years leading up to 1940, the Labour, Liberal and Agrarian parties joined in support of the defence policy.

The great powers' play for Norway

In September 1939, Germany launched a lightning attack on Poland. Great Britain and France stood behind the Poles and declared war on Hitler. The Second World War had begun.

The government announced that Norway would remain strictly neutral and instituted a border defence force on the model of the 1914 one. All the navy, air force and anti-aircraft units were called up, but only parts of the coastal defences and a few army units were put on a war footing.

After the outbreak of war the French government expressed a desire to begin military operations in Scandinavia. It wanted to engage Hitler in remote areas so that the pressure on France itself would be relieved. Also a Franco-British expedition to the north would satisfy calls from the opposition in the French National Assembly for a more active campaign. The French, too, were very preoccupied with stop-

In 1934 Adolf Hitler visited the Norwegian fjords with several of his senior officers.

ping Swedish iron ore exports to German war industries. Most of the ore was shipped via Narvik in northern Norway.

With the exception of Winston Churchill, the First Lord of the Admiralty, the British government was initially rather lukewarm about the French proposals. But during the winter of 1939–40 the British became keener on taking action as well. They saw with rising anxiety that German ships were evading the British naval blockade in the North Sea by sailing through the neutral channel along the Norwegian coast. In London dissatisfaction with the Norwegian policy of neutrality heightened considerably in December 1939, when three British merchant ships were torpedoed within the Norwegian three-mile limit. After this the British gave the Norwegians to understand that they would allow naval vessels to operate in Norwegian territorial waters. The Norwegians protested, but to no effect. In February 1940 British words became deeds. The British destroyer *Cossack* attacked the German merchant vessel *Altmark*, which had sought sanctuary in Jøssingfjord near Egersund. *Altmark* was carrying around 300 British prisoners of war. Seven Germans lost their lives when the British boarded the ship and released the prisoners.

After the Soviet Union had attacked Finland in November 1939, the British and French began planning a military campaign in the north. They decided to land troops at Narvik, troops which were then to move eastwards and take control of the iron ore mines at Kiruna and help the Finns in their winter war. The Western Allies assumed that the Germans would try to prevent such a development, and so they set up a largish force that would land at Trondheim, Bergen and Stavanger to secure bases against German counter-offensives. The operations were cancelled in the middle of March 1940 when Finland signed a peace agreement with the Soviet Union.

This decision caused Daladier's government in France to fall. The new government increased pressure on the British to organise a new campaign in Scandinavia. After some tough negotiations they agreed to laying mines close to the Norwegian coast on 8 April. The idea was that the minefields would force German shipping out into international waters, where it would be easier to attack. Simultaneously a military force was assembled in Britain which could be sent to Norway if it became obvious that the Germans were going to counter this by landing on the Norwegian coast. The British thought that the chances of such a counter-offensive were slender.

During the first months of the war, German naval command tried in vain to convince Hitler that they needed to take bases on the Norwegian coast. The navy feared it would become trapped in the Baltic. It wanted more chance of attacking Britain and wished to gain control of the North Atlantic.

It was only after the leader of the National Unity Party, Vidkun Quisling, had visited Berlin in December 1939 that Hitler gave orders to his military leaders to find out how Germany could occupy Norway. During a conversation with Hitler, Quisling had proposed that Norwegians and Germans ought to unite to fight the Jews and Communists. Such arguments may have influenced Hitler because they fitted into his ideological vision of creating a Pan-Germanic Nazi Europe united against the Communist Soviet Union.

The *Altmark* affair had convinced Hitler that Norway was unable to defend its neutrality. His invasion preparations went into a much higher gear, and in the beginning of March 1940 the operations against Denmark and Norway were given top priority. On 3 April 1940 the first ships of the invasion fleet set sail from German ports heading north. The date of attack had been fixed for 9 April.

War and occupation

1940–1945

The campaign of 1940

On 9 April the Germans occupied their objectives along the Norwegian coast. The element of surprise was great and the resistance small. Only the fortress of Oscarsborg outside Oslo gave the attackers serious problems. The fortress opened fire and destroyed the cruiser *Blücher*. Aboard were a number of key personnel and special units which were to have taken control of the capital. The sinking of the ship allowed the King, the government and parliament to get away, fleeing first to Elverum. There the *Storting* empowered the government to make decisions alone until the country was liberated.

Nevertheless, the Germans had grounds to be satisfied with the attack on Norway from a military point of view. For the first time in the history of warfare, army, navy and air force had all taken part in a combined operation in which soldiers and equipment were transported in planes and ships. The superior fire power of automatic weapons, tanks, artillery and bombers smashed all resistance.

Despite this superiority the government decided to fight. Once it had been forced to take sides, it decided to take Great Britain's part. Furthermore, a negotiated settlement with the Germans was out of the question once Vidkun Quisling proclaimed himself prime minister in a coup and Hitler had decided to support him. The government put its faith in the Allies who promised to come to the rescue.

German soldiers advancing during the battles of Valdres in April 1940.

A Norwegian soldier with a Krag-Jørgensen rifle during the campaign of 1940.

British forces landed at Åndalsnes and later at Namsos, where they got support from the French chasseur-alpin, but the efforts of the Western Allies' soldiers had little effect. There were too few of them, they lacked training and good equipment. The fiasco of these reinforcements led to a crisis in the British government which ended with Winston Churchill taking over the premiership from Neville Chamberlain.

After three weeks the Germans had gained control of southern Norway, but battle continued in the area around Narvik. Here the British, French, Polish and Norwegian troops managed to drive the Germans out of the city and isolate them in a mountainous area near the Swedish border. This was the first successful land-based military operation conducted by Allied troops during the Second World War. Even though the German units were being beaten, the Allied war leaders decided to abandon the siege at the beginning of June. Hitler's attack on France and the Benelux countries made it necessary to transfer troops to the Continent.

On 7 June 1940, the royal family and the government left for Britain to continue the fight from there. It was to be five years before they could return to a liberated Norway.

The German policy of occupation

The Germans wanted to set up an administrative organ in collaboration with the government as they had done in Denmark. This plan had to be abandoned because they had failed to capture the government and royal family. In addition, Quisling's government by coup had increased resentment, and after only a week it was replaced by an Administrative Council (*Administrasjonsrådet*) which looked after the civil administration in the occupied areas. The Supreme Court appointed the Council, which was made up of representatives of the national administration and the big industrial organisations. At the same time, Hitler set up a "*Reichskommissariat*" headed by Josef Terboven, which was the German occupation's nucleus of power for the entire war. Terboven commenced negotiations with representatives of the Administrative Council, the Supreme Court, large organisations and leading members of the *Storting*. The aim was to replace Nygaardsvold's government with a Council of State (*Riksråd*) which was to be acknowledged by the *Storting*. There was a general belief that Germany was in the process of winning the war, so the

Norwegian negotiators were as accommodating as possible, but they refused to buckle to the German demands.

In September 1940 Hitler decided that discussions were at an end. The Administrative Council was dissolved, and all parties except the National Unity Party were outlawed. Terboven proclaimed that the King and government had been removed and replaced by a new commissarial Council of State dominated by National Unity Party members. The National Unity Party under Quisling now got the chance to begin a Nazi revolution.

All through the war Norway figured large in Germany's military plans. Hitler described the country as a "fateful area" which could decide the war. He feared an Allied invasion in the north and constructed strong defensive positions all along the coast. At their most numerous the forces of occupation stood at around 430,000 men.

King Haakon VII and Crown Prince Olav photographed during an air raid outside Molde. The King's unequivocal "no" to collaboration with the invaders was an important pillar of the Norwegian resistance movement.

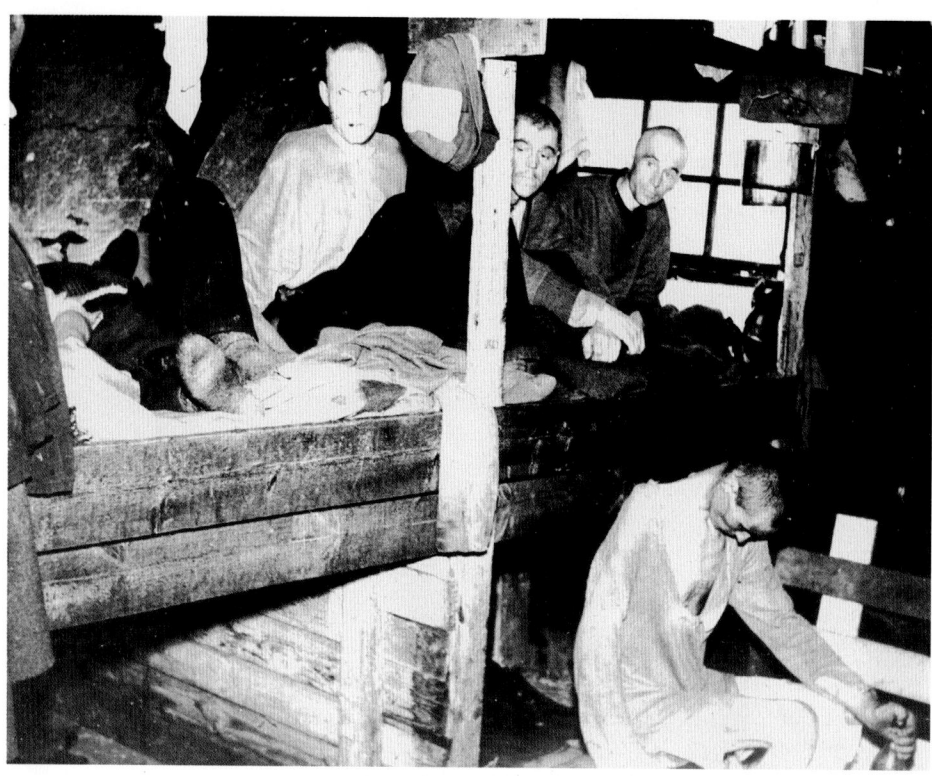

Soviet prisoners of war in a slave labour camp in northern Norway.

Norway was an important deployment area in the war against the Soviet Union, and from airfields and naval bases the Germans launched fierce attacks on the convoy routes in the North Atlantic.

German war industries made good use of Norwegian metals. The aircraft industry secured supplies of aluminium and magnesium, while the ammunition factories had good access to pyrites. In addition, the Germans took control of large amounts of fresh fish and the canning of fish products.

Although the Germans did not treat the Norwegian civilian population with the same degree of brutality as the inhabitants of other occupied areas, the war years were marked by a political repression and violence unparalleled in modern Norwegian history. Roughly 2,000 members of the resistance lost their lives after the conclusion of the hostilities of 1940. More than 30,000 people were imprisoned, and around 8,000 were sent to prisoner of war camps in Germany. Amongst these were 760 Jews, of whom only twenty-five survived. In the slave camps for Russian, Polish and Serbian prisoners of war, both German and Norwegian Nazis could give vent to their racist views. More than 17,000 prisoners succumbed to undernourishment, disease and maltreatment. Many were also executed.

Collaboration with the Germans

Support for the National Unity Party in the 1930s was principally due to the crisis in the economy, a fear of Communism, and dissatisfaction with parliamentary democracy. When the party got its historic chance during the war, about 55,000 people joined the party. Many of them were convinced that it was right to join the fight against the Communist Soviet Union, and that Germany would be the ultimate victor; around 7,000 Norwegians served under the Germans on the Eastern Front and 800 to 1,000 of them were killed. When the Nazis took over the national and local administration, a number of officials chose National Unity Party membership in order to keep their jobs. Some young people felt attracted by the party's militarism and radical programme, while others joined simply because their parents had.

But collaboration with the occupying forces was not limited to National Unity Party members. Many firms undertook contracts for the Germans, and thousands of workers had jobs in German plants. More than 9,000 Norwegian women had children by German soldiers.

The home front

Quisling's aim was to gain control of public administration. At the same time he wanted to take over national institutions, which were to be subordinated to a *Riksting* along fascist lines. Furthermore, he wanted a peace agreement between Norway and Germany which would secure the country a place in a "Pan-Germanic" Europe. As part of these plans he wanted to establish a Norwegian army to fight alongside the Germans in the war.

Nazification ended in fiasco. A widespread civil resistance movement grew up once people realised that the most basic of human rights were at stake. In the autumn of 1940 the Supreme Court resigned. The Athletics' Association's governing body withdrew, and athletics' association members boycotted all official events in protest at a Nazi reorganisation of the athletics movement. Shortly after, the

Vidkun Quisling waves to his supporters from the balcony of the Grand Hotel in Oslo in February 1942 after he had formed a new coalition government with the Germans.

bishops distanced themselves from the new authorities, and in the spring of 1941 a number of workers' organisations followed suit. That September Terboven declared a state of emergency in Oslo in an attempt to break the civil resistance. Two trade union officials were shot, and the leaders of the Norwegian Federation of Trade Unions and the Employers' Confederation were replaced with National Unity Party people. This led the membership to resign from the Nazified unions and set up secret organisations.

Civil resistance came to a head in 1942. Teachers refused to join the Nazi league of teachers and tens of thousands of parents overwhelmed the authorities with protest letters. They did not want their young people organised into a National Socialist Youth Movement. The Germans began a mass arrest of teachers, but this only helped to strengthen dissent, and the National Unity Party had to give up its schools' offensive. This defeat was a crucial factor in the failure of German trust in the National Unity Party's ability to create a National Socialist revolution in Norway. After the autumn of 1942 Hitler viewed Quisling with mistrust.

Gradually, and with close ties to the government in London,

organised resistance grew up. Towards the end of the war the Home Front's leadership managed to prevent young Norwegians from being called up for German labour and war service. This doused Quisling's hopes of forming a national army.

Members of The National Unity Party's *hird* on the march. Their black uniforms proved highly provocative to many anti-Nazis.

It was only in the final phase of the war that the military aspect of resistance came to the fore. It took time to build up a secret army (*Milorg*) that was capable of achieving anything. Initially many had feared German reprisals. Arms and equipment had to be smuggled in from abroad, and the men needed training.

In 1943 military and civil resistance began to be co-ordinated by the Home Front leadership. In the same year *Milorg* established a relationship of trust with the government in London and the Allied military command. In 1944 and 1945 Home Front forces carried out several sabotage attacks on railways and fuel depots. However, actions such as these did not dominate military resistance. The Allies gave orders that *Milorg* should hold itself in readiness in case of an invasion. Norwegian Communists criticised this strategy of preparedness; they campaigned for guerrilla warfare and carried out a number of sabotage raids on their own.

The ship *Siranger* was
torpedoed by the German
U-boat U155 in the
Atlantic on 24 October
1943.

The Foreign Front

London became the hub of Norwegian resistance abroad. The Nygaardsvold government immediately took control of the merchant fleet and welded it into the "world's biggest shipping line", *Nortraship*. The vessels were put to work transporting all kinds of supplies for the Allies and became one of Britain's lifelines. But this came at a price: 570 ships were sunk, and more than 4,500 seamen lost their lives.

The income from shipping made it possible for the government-in-exile to build up military units. Norwegian naval vessels took part in the war in the Atlantic and the North Sea. Pilots were trained in Canada and took part in the battles in the skies over Britain and the Continent. Army units were established in Scotland and Sweden. These were to be used in any invasion of Norway.

During the early years of the war the relationship between Norway and Sweden was very tense. The Swedish government had permitted the transit of German troops and materials and did not even recognise the government-in-exile until 1943. Refugees were sent back to Norway in their hundreds, and the Swedish authorities

censored any support of the Norwegian resistance campaign. Only when the fortunes of war turned against Germany did the Swedes change their policy towards Norway. They ceased turning refugees away and allowed Norwegian military units to be formed in their country. In addition they increased their humanitarian relief effort.

Vadsø was razed to the ground after the German destruction of Finnmark and north Troms. The picture shows some of the inhabitants celebrating liberation on 8 May 1945.

The government-in-exile supported the resistance movement with money, weaponry and equipment. It also took great trouble to raise morale on both the Home and Foreign Fronts. The indefatigable efforts of King Haakon and Crown Prince Olav added extra weight to the government. They were constantly on the move encouraging seamen and soldiers. They also kept up the spirits of their people back in Norway by broadcasting speeches on the radio, and they represented Norway's views to the Allies.

Liberation

The population of northern Norway was hardest hit by the ravages of war. Bodø and Narvik were severely damaged in 1940, and in 1944 eastern Finnmark was subjected to terrific Soviet bombing campaigns. That autumn, the Soviet Union wrested control of the north, and the Germans were forced to evacuate Finnmark and northern Troms. On their way south they burnt more than 10,000 houses and destroyed boats, roads, bridges and harbours. At the same time they put the inhabitants to flight. But not everyone had been forcefully evacuated. Those who had managed to conceal themselves met Soviet forces with jubilation when they entered eastern Finnmark in October 1944.

In the spring of 1945 there were still 360,000 Germans in the country and everyone feared huge damage and loss of life if they refused to surrender. It was therefore a matter of great relief when the Germans laid down their weapons on 8 May 1945.

When the peace came, a major prosecution of collaborators began. Almost 53,000 people were sentenced for treason, and of these about 23,000 were sent to prison. Quisling and twenty-four other Norwegians were executed, and twelve Germans were shot as war criminals.

The war left scars that were clearly visible in the decades immediately after liberation. Amongst those who had taken part in the war, seamen were an especially susceptible group. Many suffered psychological problems for the rest of their lives, and it was a long time before they got a decent war pension. Families affected by the prosecutions could also experience problems because it was not easy to shake off the Nazi label.

The fight against Nazi dictatorship raised the prestige of free, elected institutions, while class differences lessened. The war economy had enabled farmers, fishermen and local councils to pay off their debts, and the unemployed to find work. At the same time, the resistance campaign had forged a national cohesion which was to be very valuable when the country had to be rebuilt.

In the areas of defence and foreign policy, the war years were a turning point. The German attack demolished the policies of neutrality and disarmament, and collaboration with the Allies laid a solid foundation for closer links with the Western powers after 1945.

Ecstatic Oslo citizens celebrate the end of the war on 8 May 1945.

BYGG LANDET!

TRYGG SEIREN

DET NORSKE ARBEIDERPARTI

From liberation to EC conflict

Agreement on common values

The battle against Nazism had brought people closer together, and the enormous work of reconstruction strengthened this cohesion. This was most clearly expressed in 1945, when all the political parties went to the polls with the same political manifesto, the Joint Programme (*Fellesprogrammet*). It had a clear social democratic bias and plainly showed that the Labour Party had gained an ideological advantage over the non-socialist parties.

The Joint Programme gave the state overall responsibility for social development. The foundations for the mixed economic system that Norway has had since 1945 were being laid. In co-operation with private industry, the state would pave the way to a strong economic growth that would give people rising living standards and social stability. The Programme also stressed the reduction of unemployment and redistribution of wealth.

As in most other European countries, the war had a radicalising effect on the population. At the election in the autumn of 1945 the Labour Party got an absolute majority, and in the twenty years that followed the party dominated political development under the leadership of Einar Gerhardsen.

Reconstruction and economic growth

When the war ended, many people believed the country would be hit by a depression, like the one after the Great War. This did not hap-

An election poster used by the Labour Party during the general election in the autumn of 1945.

pen. 1945 saw the take off of an extraordinary economic growth which was to give Norway a place amongst the wealthy, industrialised nations of the world.

Reconstruction went ahead faster than expected. National product and industrial production had both passed pre-war levels by 1946, and until 1950 Norwegian economic growth was the highest in Europe. The government used rationing to limit private consumption and put emphasis on investing in production to give the country plenty of export income. This meant, for example, that imports of ships and machines came before that of bananas and private cars.

The huge demand for new production equipment from abroad took the country into a severe currency crisis in 1947. In this regard, American Marshall Aid arrived at just the right moment. From 1948 Norway received around 400 million dollars of support. The money was not only for materials and machines; the Americans arranged study trips so that Norwegian companies could gain an insight into modern industrial technology and rationalisation. In 1960 industrial productivity was 70% higher than in 1948.

The period between 1945 and 1973 was another golden age for shipping. By 1968 Norwegian ships made up about 10% of the world fleet. Over half of the ships were large tankers, but several shipowners also commissioned specialised vessels like container ships and car freighters. The number of seamen reached its peak of around 57,000 on the mid-1960s. From that point on, seamen as a group gradually declined, mainly because of rapid fleet modernisation and the increased use of foreign crew.

The active state

During the reconstruction the Labour Party borrowed from the experiences of the British and American war economies, where public planning had been used to produce weapons and equipment. Rationing was maintained, and the strict controls on foreign trade, prices and wages continued. The authorities had to approve all building and repair work and could even dictate what was to be made in factories.

Private industry acquiesced to such official sanctions while reconstruction made them necessary, but when the government put forward legislation that would make this kind of economic control possible *after* reconstruction had ended, hackles were raised. Strong resistance from the non-socialist parties and the Federation of Norwegian

NORSKE VARER
GJENNEM
MARSHALL-PLANEN

Industry forced the Labour Party to rescind the bills in 1953.

Just after the war, the Labour Party took the initiative in building new nationalised heavy industrial concerns. The most significant of these were the State Ironworks at Mo i Rana and the aluminium works in Årdal and at Sunndalsøra. However, such enterprises were never a main plank in the party's industrial policy; state support of private companies was more important. Good examples are the North of Norway Plan (*Nord-Norge-planen*) of 1951 and the Regional Development Fund (*Distriktenes Utbyggingsfond*) of 1960, which enabled the state to transfer large amounts to industry in the

Norwegian shops were filled with goods that were produced with machines and materials from American Marshall Aid.

Prime Minister Einar Gerhardsen enjoyed a unique relationship with the voters because of his modest manner, simple lifestyle and his ability to communicate with ordinary people.

Opposite page:
This family moved into one of the new housing co-operatives' flats that were built in Oslo in 1948.

regions. The same thing happened with the help of special agreements between the state and the large organisations within agriculture and fisheries.

The Labour Party was keen to develop power stations and communications. In 1950, 420,000 people were without electricity. Twenty years later the figure for those without electric power had fallen to around one thousand. By that time, too, most of the railway network had been electrified.

Although industry had more elbow room during the 1950s, this did not mean that the Labour Party had given up its desire to control economic development. The party hired economists to get some idea of the country's resources of labour, raw materials, and means of production. These new departmental experts worked on national budgets and long-term plans for synchronising public and private interests for the common good.

During the 1950s the Labour Party depended ever more heavily on macro-economic control of the economy, even though direct state intervention in the individual firm had to make way for indirect methods. The state preferred using taxes and tariffs to influence supply and demand. For example, there was a lot of duty on private cars so that the country could save currency, and subsidies administered through the national budget kept food prices down so that wage demands would be modest. The government also held the interest rate down to stimulate investment in industry, and got the

Storting to pass legislation that gave the state authority to limit the loans made by private banks. New national banks, like the State Housing Bank (*Husbanken*), the State Educational Loan Fund (*Lånekassen for Studerende Ungdom*) and the Post Office Savings Bank (*Postsparebanken*), provided the government with better opportunities to control the way borrowed money was used.

Welfare and stability

The war bonded people together in such a way that when it ended there was widespread agreement that the class warfare and want of the inter-war years must not return. Many of the ideas behind the new welfare state came from the British "Beveridge Plan". Now it would not only be society's losers who benefited from public aid; everyone would have the right to support if they found themselves in a situation of insecurity or poverty. The aim was that welfare would be financed and co-ordinated in a National Insurance scheme, but in the 1950s politicians gave a higher priority to matters such as defence and building power stations.

Because the country's economy improved faster than expected, the *Storting* did nevertheless get the opportunity to provide a social safety net, and its mesh gradually got finer. Child Allowance began in 1946, providing everyone who had children under fifteen with permanent monthly financial assistance. During the 1950s health insurance was made compulsory for all, and means-testing for the old age pension ceased. In 1964 the Social Care Act came into force which gave local council social services departments new responsi-

Stein Eriksen was one of the Norwegian athletes who won medals at the Winter Olympics in Oslo in 1952. He got a gold in the giant slalom and a silver in the slalom.

bilities. They were no longer merely to give support to the needy, but to ensure that people were able to help themselves.

A new electric express service was inaugurated on the Oslo-Stavanger railway in 1949. The last steam locomotives were withdrawn in 1970.

The balance of power between the parties did not alter much during the 1950s and 1960s. This political stability rested on the spirit of community from the war and the reconstruction. In addition the country had the benefit of good international trading conditions. The mass unemployment of the inter-war years had gone, and the great majority of people were able to experience increasing material prosperity and social security. This implied that the main aims of the Joint Programme had been achieved, and the Labour Party got the credit for it.

Western leanings

In contrast to the inter-war years, the period after 1945 was characterised by broad agreement on defence and foreign policy. Gradually, as the relationship between the superpowers deteriorated, fear of the Soviet Union increased, and the Labour Party joined with the non-socialists in a common front against the Norwegian Communists.

In the first two years after liberation, Norway had trusted that the new international body, the UN, would ensure peace. The government wished to play an active, bridge-building role in the international community. Norway would avoid bloc politics and steer clear of military alliances. At the same time everyone agreed they wanted a beefed-up national defence.

The foundations of this bridge-building policy soon began to crumble. During 1947 a deep rift opened up between East and West, as the Soviet Union tightened its grip on Eastern Europe, while the USA promised military and economic assistance to states that felt themselves threatened from the east. Collaboration between the super-powers at the UN stagnated. The Cold War had arrived. In such a situation it was impossible for Norway to play any kind of active mediating role; the country was too weak both economically and militarily. As a result, Norway's UN policy was both passive and cautious.

Most Norwegians had considerable sympathy for the Soviet Union after the liberation of Finnmark. But even as early as the autumn of 1946 a change of attitude had begun to occur. When Norway's large neighbour in the east demanded joint Norwegian-Soviet military bases on Spitzbergen, Norwegian suspicions were aroused. Accordingly, the government rejected the demands and strengthened its military co-operation with the Western powers. Most Norwegian arms purchases were made in Great Britain, and from 1947 Norway took part in the occupation of Germany under British command. At the same time the ties with British and American intelligence were strengthened.

Norway made an important move to the West in 1947 when the government decided to participate in the Marshall Plan. The decision was easy: Norway's leading trade partners were doing the same, and the lack of foreign currency was acute.

The coup in Czechoslovakia in 1948 unleashed a wave of anti-Communist sentiment. Prime Minister Einar Gerhardsen led the crusade against the "peril in our midst". The Norwegian Communist Party were now branded as Soviet fifth columnists who "deep down" were "supporters of terror and dictatorship". The campaign led to mass resignations from the party, and internal dissent weakened the Communists' effectiveness. The situation was not improved by the party supporting the Soviet Union during the Cold War and adopting a more revolutionary course. Within a short time the Norwegian Communist Party had been reduced to an isolated rump.

When differences between East and West increased in 1948, negotiations began between Norway, Sweden and Denmark for a Nordic defence pact. The discussions got nowhere, however; Sweden wanted an independent alliance, whereas Norway wanted to have links with the West for weapons deliveries and a clear guarantee of aid in the event of war, all of which had to be planned for in peace time.

After the collapse of the Nordic talks, the idea began to gain ground that only NATO membership could provide the country with security. There was considerable scepticism for this view within the Labour Party, but when the Prime Minister overcame his doubts, other objectors fell silent. In the spring of 1949 a solid majority of the *Storting* voted to join this new Western defence alliance.

After joining NATO, the government was keen to mollify the Soviet Union. In what was called the "bases declaration" Norway made it clear that she would not allow the permanent stationing of foreign troops or atomic weapons on Norwegian soil in peace time. In the ensuing years, restrictions on military activity in Finnmark were also imposed, a policy that was meant to prevent the Soviet Union from increasing pressure on Finland.

The bases policy did not prevent NATO forces from taking part in short-term operations on Norwegian territory, and the Norwegian authorities never checked whether Allied ships had atomic weapons aboard when they visited the country. As well as this the military built early warning stations and weapons' dumps for Allied reinforcements, and procured planes and rockets that could be equipped with atomic weapons in an emergency. From the late 1950s American spy planes operated from Norwegian airfields. The flights took place without the sanction of the government, and they first officially came to light when a U2 plane on its way to Bodø was shot down over the Soviet Union in 1960.

In the 1950s Norway put collaboration with the USA and Great Britain above that with Scandinavia and Western Europe. Economic policy was co-ordinated within the Organisation for European Economic Co-operation (OEEC) which promoted free trade. As a consequence, Norway had to allow more imports and concentrate on the goods and services that the country had a natural capacity for – like aluminium and shipping.

USA.   USSR.
STANS KAPPLØPET MOT DØDEN
LIVET KREVER TILLIT

An anti-nuclear weapons demonstration outside the *Storting* in 1961.

Norway turned down plans for a Nordic tariff union and adopted a critical attitude towards Common Market co-operation, as Norwegian industry feared competition from Swedish factories and Danish farming. Many Norwegian politicians were also equivocal about supranational organisations. It was 1960 before Norwegian industry began to launch out seriously into international competition, when Norway joined the Western European, British dominated free trade association, EFTA, which got its members to lower tariffs, but had no supranational authority, lacked any common external tariff barriers and did not cover agriculture and fisheries.

It was only within the labour movement that small pockets of resistance continued to fight NATO. They protested about rearmament and were unhappy that the Labour leadership tried to prevent open discussion of foreign and defence issues. They were also opposed to the way the Labour Party was becoming less socialist and more amenable towards private industry.

At the end of the 1950s opponents of NATO took an active role in the Western European campaign against atomic weapons. When the 1961 annual Labour Party Conference agreed that atomic weapons could be sited on Norwegian soil if there was a threat of war, many on the Left had had enough. Some of the most discontented founded the Socialist People's Party (*Sosialistisk Folkeparti*).

Its manifesto demonstrated that the old ideas from between the wars – of neutrality and disarmament – were not dead, and the very founding of the party was in itself a sign that the coldest period of the Cold War was over. To everyone's astonishment the Socialist People's Party managed to win two *Storting* seats in the general election of 1961. Now the Labour Party had got a troublesome competitor on its left flank.

Nordic collaboration

Although attempts to create a Scandinavian tariff union and a Nordic defence agreement came to nothing, the ties between the Scandinavian countries were strengthened after the war. In 1952 the parliaments of Sweden, Denmark, Iceland and Norway voted to establish a new co-operative body, which Finland joined three years later. The Nordic Council (*Nordisk Råd*) consists of parliamentarians and members of government who meet once a year to discuss matters of common interest. The assembly cannot produce binding legislation, but the Council's recommendations have usually been implemented. In the 1950s the use of passports between Nordic countries was discontinued, and a common labour market was established that entitled workers who had crossed their joint boundaries to the same social security benefits as Norwegian citizens. The Council's greatest importance was as a place of contact, where Scandinavian politicians could pool ideas and experience.

The Nordic countries co-operated closely within the UN. As small nations they found it easier to be heard by the bigger powers if they stood together on common interest issues. It was also usual for Scandinavian military units to operate closely in peace-keeping operations.

The Scandinavian airline SAS was created in 1946 with the governments of Sweden, Denmark and Norway as majority sharehold-

A Norwegian-built shrimp trawler off the Indian state of Kerala in 1960.

ers. The company was a success, but did not become a model for Scandinavian projects in the future. It was only after the Nordic countries became members of the free trade association EFTA that their economic links were seriously exploited.

Norway and the Third World. From Kerala to NORAD

Norway was one of the first countries to inaugurate bilateral development programmes. As early as 1952 the *Storting* granted money for an Indo-Norwegian fishery project in Kerala. The initiative came from the Labour leadership, which wanted to give their NATO critics something else to think about, though there were other factors at play when the *Storting* designed the first aid programmes. A number of politicians wanted to use Third World help to stem the tide of Communism, while others stressed the importance of Christian charity and a commitment to the world's poor. In 1962 India Aid (*Indiahjelpen*) was superseded by Norwegian Development Aid (*Norsk utviklingshjelp*), which changed its name to NORAD six years later.

As a proportion of gross national product, Norway's development aid was amongst the most substantial in the world. Roughly half the money was given to several extremely poor major partners in Asia and Africa. The remainder went into the UN system and to private aid organisations that gave humanitarian aid. The aim of Norwegian aid was to improve the lot of the average man or woman. In the main it was made in the form of gifts – not loans – and very little was tied to the supply of Norwegian goods and services.

The "golden" Sixties

The period from 1960 to 1973 was a golden age for industry which benefited from good international trading conditions and did well in the tough competitive atmosphere engendered by free trade within EFTA. Foreign investment increased sharply, particularly in power-consuming industry. By the end of the 1960s Norway was the largest European exporter of aluminium and the world's largest exporter of ferro-alloys.

This large growth in industry had knock-on effects in the commodities, transport and construction industries. It was hardly surprising that the demand for labour increased. Fortunately there was a reserve that could be tapped. During the 1960s more and more married women went out to work. Many wanted to increase the family income to be able to purchase new consumer durables, and the fact that women on average had fewer children than before made it easier to go out to work. In addition, new contraceptives such as the pill and the coil arrived, and these made it very easy for women to choose whether they wanted to have children or not.

The symbol of this new cornucopia was the private car. After October 1960 it was no longer necessary to apply for permission to buy a car, and in the next few years, thousands of proud car owners took to the roads. Driving enthusiasm was not dented despite a dramatic rise in road accidents.

1960 also saw the official opening of Norwegian television, and over the course of the 1960s around 900,000 Norwegians got television sets. As most of them could only receive one channel, the Norwegian Broadcasting Corporation, the programmes fostered an extraordinary cultural cohesion amongst the population. This had a palpable effect on daily life until the introduction of cable television and satellite dishes in the 1980s, which increased the choice of programmes.

Non-socialist shift

Because the Labour Party was moving towards the political centre, it was necessary for the non-socialist parties to mark their own individual territory, and old fault lines were kept open. The Christian People's Party in particular was keen to display its character. The party had made its breakthrough as a new, national and non-socialist alternative in 1945. It wanted to be seen as a guardian of Christian morality – with a "message from God" – above class division and party politics. The Christian People's Party worked frantically, but in vain, to halt the Labour Party's resolution to strengthen state responsibility for sex education and contraception. The party did, however, win through in trying to stop the reduction in Christian education at school, and led the campaign against abortion on social grounds.

The Centre Party stood for provincial Norway and the interests of agriculture and could easily find itself in conflict with the Conservatives, which represented city culture and had close ties with industry and shipping. The Liberal Party was divided into social-liberal and liberal wings. The social-liberal part, which gained the ascendancy in the 1950s, had sympathy with the Labour Party's economic policies and was sceptical of the Christian People's Party's attitude to cultural issues. Early in the 1960s the question of Norwegian participation in the Common Market also caused co-operative difficulties for the non-socialist parties. The Conservatives wanted full membership, the Centre Party was against, whilst the Liberals and Christian People's Party were split. It was only after de Gaulle, the French President, had vetoed enlargement of the Community in 1963, that the parties could join together against the Labour government.

The election of 1961 had given the Labour Party and the non-socialists an equal number of seats in the *Storting*, while the Socialist People's Party had two seats. It meant that the Labour government would have to step down if the Socialist People's Party and the non-socialists agreed on a vote of no confidence. This was precisely what happened in 1963, when discontent with the Labour Party's industrial policy brought the non-socialists to power.

Although the Conservative government of John Lyng was top-
pled by the Labour Party and the Socialist People's Party after only
three weeks, it was of great psychological significance. The forming of
a government brought the non-socialists closer together and helped
them reach agreement on a common political manifesto. At the election in the autumn of 1965, the Conservative, Liberal, Christian
People's and Centre parties got a clear majority in the *Storting*. Now
the Centre Party's Per Borten could form a non-socialist government.

The Borten government followed the same general line as the
Labour Party, and the Welfare State and other aspects of public
works were developed still further. This cost money, and taxes rose.
This non-socialist government brought in compulsory nine-year
schooling, VAT and National Insurance.

The British Ferguson tractor revolutionised the work on many farms in the 1950s.

Centralisation

Although Norway did not experience the same urban growth as the
Continent, there was an unparalleled migration of people after 1945.
At the end of the war, roughly half the population lived in towns and

communities of more than two hundred inhabitants. Twenty-five
years later this figure had risen to about two thirds. But migration
did not lead to whole areas becoming depopulated as happened in
Sweden and Finland.

Agricultural mechanisation took a new leap forward in the 1950s.
At the same time the *Storting* passed laws that could protect farmers
against foreign competition, and channelled large amounts of money
into agricultural subsidies. This was partly done to slow urban migration down, but the subsidies were also to ensure that the country was
not over dependent on food imports. At the start of the 1970s, state
subsidies to farming were above average for OECD countries; only
Switzerland and Japan gave greater subsidies than Norway.

During the 1930s fishermen had forced through a law forbidding the construction of new trawlers. They feared that modern
boats would deprive them of their livelihood at a time of high unemployment. In the post-war era the situation had changed. Politicians
now agreed that fisheries had to be streamlined, and that catches
should be processed by filleting factories, cold storage plants, fish

meal processors and fish oil factories. This would increase the country's export revenue. The fish processing companies wanted – and got – deliveries from new trawlers that did long distance fishing and could ensure supplies all year round.

Modernisation of the fishing industry led to a continuous fall in the number of fishermen. Particularly those who combined farming with fishing, left the sea, and many of them also decided to leave their small farms.

The education explosion and youth revolt

The extension of elementary education made it possible for increasing numbers of young people to enter higher education. Pupil numbers at grammar and vocational schools rose sharply, and universities and colleges were flooded with students. 1968 saw the opening of new universities in Trondheim and Tromsø, and the following year the building of regional colleges began.

In common with young people in other Western countries, sections of the Norwegian teenage population turned a critical eye on their parents' affluence in the 1960s. The Anglo-American pop industry got a firm foothold and provided young people with new fashions and ideals. Long hair and blue jeans were signs that a distinct youth culture was growing up. Social conventions became less formal, and respect for authority of all kinds diminished. Television gave teenagers a new view of the world: they were the first to be able to watch live coverage of famines and battlefields in their own living rooms. The media shock often caused frustration and rootlessness amongst the young. Some also reacted to adult materialism and get-ahead mentality.

When universities became oversubscribed with students, the authorities suggested that the old, unstructured studies should be replaced by teaching plans that had rigid courses and more exams. Behind these suggestions lay the desire to make courses shorter and more relevant to the needs of economic life. The students went on strike and demonstrated to retain open, socially critical studies. Inspired by the spirit of revolt in American and European universities, the students attacked the authoritarian university faculties. Their protests paid dividends. The students were given places on the governing bodies of universities and a say in deciding the content of courses.

The American war in Vietnam aroused sympathy for developing countries. Many young people saw the war as a sign that rich countries had the main responsibility for want and lack of freedom in the Third World.

The most alienated of the socialist students, the Marxist-Leninists, had decided that the capitalist system in Norway should be overthrown by armed revolution. For them Mao's China was the great ideal, and after some of them had given up their studies and become "proletarianised", they gained positions of influence in certain local trade unions. They led a number of "wildcat" strikes and focused attention on jobs with low pay and bad conditions.

The green revolution

During the 1960s people realised that strong economic growth had its downsides. Over-culling had led to a moratorium on Norwegian whaling in the Antarctic. Herring disappeared from the North Sea, and mackerel fishing was greatly reduced. Effluent from industry, agriculture and sewage pipes threatened life in lakes, fjords and rivers. Air pollution rose dramatically. Acid rain from Great Britain and the Continent ruined thousands of fishing lakes in southern Norway, and poisonous crop sprays upset the balance of nature. Rubbish tips proliferated. As did the need for electricity. The result was that ever more waterfalls, rivers and lakes were harnessed for power purposes. The last remaining wilderness areas of Europe were in danger of disappearing.

Pollution and the ruthless exploitation of natural resources gave impetus to environmental protection work. The Norwegian Society for the Conservation of Nature (*Norges Naturvernforbund*) took the lead in voluntary work and insisted that the authorities take action.

Way back in 1962 the *Storting* voted to turn the mountainous region of Rondane into the country's first national park, and in the ensuing years other areas were permanently protected from intrusion. But the real breakthrough for conservation came in European Natural Conservation Year in 1970. New environmental protection legislation was introduced on water pollution, and during the same year a group of environmental protesters used civil disobedience in the environmental struggle. When northern Europe's highest waterfall, Mardalsfossen, was to be exploited, they attempted to halt the construction work. The police removed the demonstrators, but the debate about hydro-electric development was now very much on the agenda. During the 1970s the *Storting* decided that several water courses should be protected against development.

Norway was the first country in the world to establish a Ministry of the Environment in 1972. Its experts drafted many laws and regulations that helped improve the environment in various areas. But national measures alone were not enough. During the 1970s and 1980s Norway redoubled her efforts to try to establish international environmental agreements.

The EC battle

In 1970 the Borten government began negotiations on Norway's entry into the European Communities (EC), but just the year after the coalition broke down because of disagreements on the European question. It was replaced by a minority government led by Trygve Bratteli of the Labour Party, who negotiated an agreement on full membership. The agreement was rejected in a referendum in 1972, and as a result had to be replaced by a free trade agreement covering industrial goods, which was signed in 1973.

Opponents of the EC had a strong dislike of handing over Norwegian sovereignty to supranational organisations in Brussels. They were also angered by the EC's plans for an economic and political union and did not like the way democratically elected bodies were given so little influence. Many had a great antipathy to the EC's philosophy of growth– a dislike that encompassed much of the criticism that had been levelled at post-war Norwegian society from the Left, from conservationists and from student protesters. Principles that dictated that goods, services, capital and labour should move freely across borders, seemed terrifying; some people feared that European big business, especially the German, would dominate the Norwegian economy. That could mean more districts suffering depopulation and the pressure on natural resources and the environment increasing. The fear of such a development was only heightened when the EC refused to give Norwegian farmers and fishermen special protection.

Opponents put together an effective popular movement that managed to gain the upper hand in the opinion polls. Its most important constituents were farmers, fishermen, left-wing socialists and radical trade unionists. They were also supported by many lay Christians, teetotallers and New Norwegian supporters.

The Yes vote was dominated by the country's governing elite. It stressed that the EC would strengthen peace, create greater economic growth and give Norway a greater say in the development of Europe. Supporters also emphasised that Norway would do well to follow the example of Britain and Denmark. But the case made by the majority of the *Storting*, with the Conservatives, the government and the Labour leadership in the vanguard, was not powerful enough, despite support from big business, the leadership of the Norwegian Federation of Trade Unions and most of the newspapers. Nor did it help when Prime Minister Bratteli threatened to resign if the electors did not follow the government's recommendation. A majority of 53% said no.

Rolf Groven's painting "Norwegian neo-romanticism" from 1972 brought out the main arguments in the Norwegian anti-EC campaign: membership would threaten the right to national autonomy, destroy the country's ecology and open it up to big business from abroad.

Norway – an oil producer

The oil adventure

In 1966 oil prospecting began in the Norwegian sector of the North Sea. Many companies joined the hunt for "black gold", but one by one they gave up. By the autumn of 1969 Phillips Petroleum Company was alone in not having lost hope. In the last hole the company decided to bore, the drill stem of the Ocean Viking rig struck an oil field. In 1970 the experts established that not only was the field economically viable, it was actually amongst the ten largest in the world. Norway had become an oil nation!

In the 1960s the *Storting* had put together a legal framework that gave the state strict control, and a large income, from oil operations. To prevent Norway becoming simply an exporter of crude oil and gas, the authorities aimed to build up a national oil industry. It would take part in prospecting, extracting and refining the resources in collaboration with foreign companies: the huge investments and high risk made it desirable to share the responsibility. The politicians gave the national oil company, Statoil, an advantageous position with a considerable stake in future finds, and the state dominated company Norsk Hydro was also to share in the adventure.

The maritime oil business could be a risky one. In 1977 there was an uncontrolled blow-out in the Ekofisk Field that caused an oil leak and a pollution alert on the Norwegian coast. Fortunately, American experts managed to stop the leak after only eight days thus avoiding an environmental catastrophe. Three years later the accommodation rig, Alexander Kielland, was completely wrecked in a storm and 123 oil workers were killed. These accidents forced the authorities to tighten

Oil workers at the Statfjord Field in the North Sea.

up on oil protection contingencies and safety rules, but did not cause any slow down in the tempo of prospecting and extraction.

The value of crude oil and gas production increased rapidly. In 1990 Norway overtook Britain as Europe's largest oil producer, and by the mid-1990s Norway had become the second largest oil exporter in the world after Saudi-Arabia.

The oil trade posed great challenges for industry and research. Norwegian engineers not only developed advanced methods of seismic oil prospecting, but also systems for horizontal oil drilling and fully automated robotic installations for oil and gas extraction on the sea bed. The most spectacular monuments to this new technology were the gigantic rigs. In the summer of 1995 the world's largest oil rig was towed out to the Troll Field, which at that time was Europe's largest maritime gas field.

In relation to investment, the oil industry did not create all that many new jobs. The new industry demanded a highly qualified labour force using modern high technology. At the start of the 1990s about 20,000 people were employed in the oil industry, about 1% of the total labour force. Many of them lived in Stavanger, which became the country's oil capital.

Statoil became a money-making machine for the Norwegian economy. The company took over the operational responsibility for large oil fields like Statfjord and Gullfaks and set up subsidiaries in other parts of the world. It also bought up filling stations in neighbouring countries, acquired refineries and became part-owner of several pipeline plants in the North Sea.

Maritime demarcation disputes in the north

As a result of international conferences on maritime law in the 1970s, Norway secured a continental shelf extending to roughly 1,5 million square kilometres and an economic zone of about two million square kilometres. No other European state, with the exception of the Soviet Union, had such large sea areas under its control. The extension of maritime territory led to a conflict with the Kremlin about the demarcation line in the Barents Sea. While awaiting a final solution, an interim agreement was reached on sharing the fish resources in the disputed areas off the Finnmark coast.

The question of the utilisation of the fishing areas surrounding Spitzbergen remained unresolved. Norway maintained that the provi-

ARCTIC OCEAN

Sector line

Mid line

Novaja Zemlja

"*Smutthullet*"

BARENTS SEA

Spitzbergen

"*The Grey Zone*"

GREENLAND

Tromsøflaket *Snøhvit*

Askeladden

Sørøya ●Hammerfest
Sletnes

RUSSIA

Jan Mayen

NORWEGIAN SEA

●Harstad

FINLAND

Træna Bank

●Sandnessjøen

Norne
Halten Bank
Heidrun
Smørbukk Midgard
Draugen

SWEDEN

ICELAND

●Tjeldbergodden
●Kristiansund

Agat ●Florø NORWAY

The Faroes
Magnus Snorre
Thistle Statfjord
Tern Gullfaks
Heather ●Sture Mongstad
Ninian Troll Kollsnes
Victory Oseberg Bergen
Claire Alwyn Frigg
Beryl Frøy
Shetland Helmdal Bamble
Balder Hermod ●Kårstø ●Slagen
The Orkneys Gudrun Stavanger
Brae Gleipner
Flotta Pipa Forties NORTH SEA
Beatrice Cod
Nigg Bay Ula Fredericia
●St Fergus Gyda
Aberdeen ●Cruden Bay Fulmar Ekofisk Nybro
Auk Valhall Tyra
Argyll Dan Emden
Teeside Uithuizen
GREAT BRITAIN

ECONOMIC ZONES
Oil and gas fields

Unregulated area

1978 Interim agreement
on fishing rights

Dividing line/economic zones

Oil field

Gas field

Oil and gas field

Condensate (liquid gas)

● Landing point

Oil pipeline

Planned oil pipeline

Gas pipeline

Planned gas pipeline

sions of the Spitzbergen Treaty giving equal rights to all signatories to exploit its natural resources, did not apply further than four nautical miles from the coast. Within the remainder of the 200 mile zone around the archipelago Norway wanted the same rights as on the continental shelf and economic zone surrounding its mainland. The international community showed little sympathy for this demand.

In 1977 Norway instituted a fish protection zone around Spitzbergen. Countries that had previously fished in the area were given quotas and were required to report their catches. Most states respected these Norwegian regulations, but the Soviet Union refused to submit reports. In 1994 Icelandic trawlers began to fish in the Spitzbergen zone. Several of the vessels were seized by the coastguard and fines were imposed by Norwegian courts. At the same time the Icelanders began fishing for cod in the Loophole (Smutthullet), an area of international water in the Barents Sea. This uncontrolled fishing ceased in 1999 when Russia, Iceland and Norway came to a quota agreement for the Loophole.

Reaching agreement with the Danes about the demarcation line between Jan Mayen and Greenland was easier. The matter was left to the International Court at the Hague which worked out a compromise in 1993.

The oil finds and the new-found sovereignty over large areas of sea increased Norway's economic and strategic importance. Rearmament on the Kola Peninsula had the same effect. The Soviet Northern Fleet's effectiveness increased during the 1970s and so did Norway's security needs. This prompted Norway and the USA to make arrangements for the advance storage of weapons for the marines, and the construction of bases for American air and naval forces.

The reforms and counter-cyclical policies of the 1970s

From 1973 to 1981 the Labour Party formed three minority governments in succession, seeking support from various parties issue by issue. They took notice of the cultural debate over the Common Market and put demands for democratisation, decentralisation and conservation on the agenda. Oil revenues gave politicians plenty of scope to carry out reforms at a time when the rest of Europe was struggling with economic recession. Legislation on industrial democracy and the working environment increased employees' influence on working practices. A new comprehensive sixth form

college replaced the old system of grammar schools, vocational schools and business schools. In 1976 the *Storting* passed an incremental plan for farmers which guaranteed them higher incomes.

Neo-feminist groups began to spring up after 1970, modelled on the American feminist movement, Women's Lib, and during the 1970s this new women's movement speeded up the work for sexual equality. Alodial law was changed in 1974. From that time on girls and boys had an equal right to inherit farms. Sexual equality legislation came in four years later. It made it illegal to discriminate between the sexes and gave a single rate for a particular job. An Equal Status Office was given the job of making sure the regulations were respected. In 1978 the women's movement won another important victory when the *Storting* passed legislation on abortion on demand.

The battle for equality led to more women holding political office and getting better places on the candidates' list. The number of women in democratically elected bodies increased considerably. A milestone was reached in 1981 when Gro Harlem Brundtland became the country's first woman prime minister.

The international recession, sparked off by the oil crisis of 1973, caused falling production and unemployment in large parts of the world. Norway was an exception. The government took out an advance on the oil billions to keep the wheels turning, and large foreign loans helped industry and shipping through the crisis. As a result, wages rose in real terms between 1974 and 1977, and unemployment was kept at bay. During this period Norway had better growth than most other OECD countries. But there was another side

When Gro Harlem Brundtland became the prime minister in 1986 her government included eight women. This was the highest proportion in any government in the world and aroused international interest.

In the 1980s and 1990s
there was a steady in-
crease of immigrant
children taking part in the
Constitution Day celebra-
tions on 17 May. This
showed that Norway was
on the way to becoming a
multi-cultural society.

to the coin. By 1977 foreign debt had risen to 100 billion kroner – more than half the national product. At the same time Norwegian goods were losing their competitive edge in the world market. The growth in wages and the standards of living had overreached itself. From the late 1970s cost cutting policies had to be introduced.

Immigration

The high economic growth of the 1960s led to a shortage of labour, and for the first time in many years Norway had an immigration surplus. The majority of immigrants came from Western Europe and the USA. Many of them were oil industry experts. However, during the 1970s the numbers of people from south-eastern Europe, Asia and Africa increased, partly as a result of Western European coun- tries closing their borders to new guest workers.

The increasing stream of unskilled labour from poor countries forced the authorities to impose stricter controls on immigration in 1975. Despite this, the number of foreigners rose in the years that followed; the oil industry was still short of skilled labour, and many immigrants exercised their rights to bring their families to Norway. In the early Eighties the country accepted several thousand Vietnamese refugees, most of whom had been picked up by Norwegian merchant ships in the South China Sea.

Immigrants from the Third World had trouble finding work and suffered unemployment more frequently than Norwegians. As a rule they had to accept low status jobs in industry and the service sector even though many of them had higher education.

Immigration put Norwegian tolerance to the test. Those who had little education and scant contact with foreign workers were espe- cially sceptical of immigrants. The most militant amongst them did not balk at destroying immigrants' shops or spreading racist propa- ganda. But such groups never gained much general support.

The numbers of asylum seekers from underdeveloped countries ravaged by war and terror began to rise by the end of the 1980s, and they moved steadily upwards towards the turn of the millennium. At the start of 2002 there were about 317,000 people with an immi- grant background living in the country. This represented 6.9% of the population. The largest constituent groups were Pakistanis, Swedes and Danes, and the majority lived in Oslo where one in five people had a foreign background.

The Sami demand their rights

After the war the authorities gave up their tough policy of Norwegianisation and announced that they wanted to protect the Sami culture, language and way of life. However, the Norwegian authorities did little to implement their new Sami policies while the Sami lacked proper organisation and a political leadership with clear cut objectives.

There were many reasons why the Sami had difficulty organising themselves. For centuries they had been discriminated against and persecuted, and, as a consequence, many of them had forsaken their roots and left the Sami heartlands. Furthermore, they were few in number, they were spread thinly across four countries and they spoke different languages.

The first ones to unite properly were the reindeer Sami who founded their own association in 1948. Sami from Sweden, Finland and Norway started a Nordic Sami association in the mid-1950s, and in 1964 the government set up the Norwegian Sami Council, which

A Sami making his protest outside the *Storting* against the development of the River Alta.

The Conservative parliamentary leader, Kåre Willoch, is cheered by a worker after the general election of 1981. During the 1980s the Conservatives gained votes from groups who had tradtionally voted Labour.

had an advisory status in Sami matters. Four years later an organisation with the aim of uniting the Sami around a common political manifesto was started. But it did not succeed in gathering the great majority of Sami within one organisation. One group quickly broke away and formed a rival association, while another believed that the Sami ought not to align themselves along ethnic lines, but work for Sami issues from inside the Norwegian political parties.

In the 1950s state grants for Sami education were improved and in the two decades which followed, educated and self-confident leaders appeared in the Sami organisations and made them more effective. Several of them drew inspiration from the work of the World Council for Indigenous Peoples (WCIP), which was founded in 1975.

The rapid industrialisation after 1945 put more pressure on the Sami culture. More and more people viewed with apprehension the way the Scandinavian majorities pushed into areas that had been under Sami control for thousands of years. When State Power Systems wanted to develop the Alta-Kautokeino watercourse in the early 1970s, patience snapped. Under the slogan "Let the river live!" the Sami together with environmental activists unified to stop the construction machines. The demonstration was supported by indigenous peoples in other parts of the world and created great international interest. In 1981 the government set large police contingents on to the demonstrators, and the building of the power station could begin.

The Alta affair forced the authorities to be more receptive to Sami demands. One result of this change of attitude was that the Sami were allowed to establish their own democratically elected body, the *Sametinget* (Sami Parliament) in 1989. In the same year the *Storting* passed a new paragraph in the Constitution that stated that the Norwegian state had a duty to protect Sami language, culture and social life. But deciding the question of Sami rights to land and lakes took longer; by the turn of the millennium these knotty questions still had not finally been resolved.

Liberalisation and the swing to the right in the 1980s

The number of voters supporting the Conservatives swelled during the 1970s, and the party had its best result to date at the 1981 election. With 31.7% of the vote it initially formed a one-party government, and then from 1983 went into a coalition with the Centre, Christian People's and Liberal parties. Both governments had the Conservatives' Kåre Willoch as prime minister.

The Willoch governments reduced taxes and allowed market forces freer play. Local government regulation of rents in private accommodation ceased, and members of housing co-operatives got the right to become owner occupiers. Foreigners got better opportunities to buy Norwegian securities and people who bought into unit trusts were given tax relief. The business at the Oslo Stock Exchange quickly reached record levels. The state broadcasting monopoly was abolished; 1982 saw the introduction of new local radio stations, and private firms began laying cable networks for local television stations and satellite television.

Private consumption increased sharply in the first half of the 1980s. This was a result of the government's deregulation of state controls on the private loan market. People purchased cars and other luxury goods on an unprecedented scale. Most of it was financed by bank loans. The banks also lent large sums to the commodity trade as well as share and property speculation.

The economic situation changed when the price of oil fell drastically and foreign currency dealers began to sell Norwegian kroner. During the winter of 1985–86, the Bank of Norway spent 28 billion kroner trying to shore up the krone rate. The budget deficit increased rapidly and the Willoch government was forced to raise taxes and cut back national expenditure. But the Progress Party (*Fremskrittspartiet*) which held the balance in the *Storting*, could not accept an increase in petrol duty. When the Labour Party agreed and demanded a vote of confidence, the government had to step down.

The Labour Party formed a minority government in the spring of 1986, led by Gro Harlem Brundtland, which sat until the elections of 1989. Then a new non-socialist government with Jan P. Syse as prime minister took over.

At the end of the 1980s the Progress Party made its breakthrough as a national party after being hampered by internal battles and low levels of support since its inception in 1972. The party's main aims were to work for "large reductions in taxes, tariffs and state interference" and it criticised the Conservatives' middle-of-the-road policies.

People who supported the Progress Party were not just fed up with high taxes: they also objected to the state and local government taking on ever more duties at an ever greater cost. Here, the party took inspiration from the neo-liberal policies of Margaret Thatcher and Ronald Reagan.

Norwegian neo-liberalism was a reaction to the welfare and redistribution policies that had been adopted since 1945. The Progress Party believed that the state had become too concerned with cocooning people and wanted the individual to be paid according to merit.

The party found sympathy amongst voters who were against state-donated international aid, and who were critical of immigration from the Third World. Those who were dubious about Women's Lib also found it easy to tick the Progress Party box during elections.

The Progress Party's leader, Carl I. Hagen, bore much of the credit for its progress. He had personal charisma, spoke simply and directly and was an impressive television performer. Hagen personified a new, fresh approach which appealed to people who had grown tired of the old parties. The party leader cleared out ultra-liberal groups and racist elements which could blur the party's profile.

After a poor result in 1993, the Progress Party made a strong comeback in the elections of 1997 and 2001, winning 25 and 26 *Storting* seats respectively.

Economy and the environment in the Oil Age

When Norway became an oil producing nation, its national economy was affected in a big way. High wages in the oil industry forced prices and wages up in the mainstream economy making it hard for sections of industry to compete internationally. Labour intensive concerns that were not very knowledge-based and produced little added value, such as shoe factories and clothing manufacturers,

Frederic Hauge and the environmental organisation Bellona played a key role in the conservation battles of the 1980s and 1990s. The organisation carried out several unlawful operations against Norwegian and foreign companies. In the picture Hauge is being arrested during the excavation of drums of toxic waste at Porsgrunn.

were especially vulnerable. The downturn in industrial employment was also linked to firms' adoption of new technology, especially computers. Additionally, jobs were lost through amalgamations.

After strongly backing state owned industry in the 1970s, the Labour Party changed its attitude in the following decade. During the swing to the Right there was less political will to support concerns that were losing money. Accordingly, a number of nationalised companies, headed by the Labour Party's old flag-ship project, the State Ironworks, were closed down.

Oil revenues gave Norway wonderful freedom of action in matters of national economy. While other OECD countries had to rein in their public sector activity, Norway was one of the nations that used the greatest percentage of GNP on public expenditure, and which had the highest proportion of its workforce employed in the public sector. The preponderance of the new jobs in this sector of the economy were created by local government, especially in the health, social and education services, and a good majority were taken by women.

The new environmental legislation had a positive effect. Harmful effluents were reduced and the water quality of rivers, fjords and lakes improved. An important victory was won in the early 1980s when Norway's largest lake, Lake Mjøsa, was saved from serious algal pollution.

But a number of problems remained unsolved. Many townspeople lacked good quality drinking water, and asphalt dust from studded tyres was a problem in cities and built-up areas. So were the enormous smoke clouds that blew in across eastern Finnmark from a nickel works in Russia. Increasing production of oil and gas caused emissions of carbon dioxide to rise, though this trend was defended by the environmental protection agencies. Their argument was that Norwegian gas exports helped to replace coal and atomic power in other countries, making the total emission of carbon dioxide in Europe fall. The environmental lobby had little patience with this view. It maintained that Norwegian gas made energy saving and renewables unprofitable.

Pollution from Great Britain and the Continent continued to affect the country. During the decade between 1980 and 1990 more lakes lost their fish because of acid rain. Analyses of tests done on deep sea fish clearly indicated that coastal sea currents were transporting far too much environmental toxin.

Thor Heyerdahl's accounts of his expeditions on the balsa wood raft Kon-Tiki and the reed boats Ra I and Ra II aroused attention and stimulated controversy in many countries. As one of Norway's few international celebrities, he took part in the opening of the Winter Olympics in Lillehammer in 1994.

Norway wanted to be a leading force in international environmental work, so it was very timely that Gro Harlem Brundtland was elected leader of the UN Commission on Environment and Development, which published the "Brundtland Report" in 1987. The Commission advanced the ambitious goal of "sustainable" development, which means that the world must strive towards a development "which satisfies today's needs without ruining the ability of future generations to satisfy their own".

Characteristics of social development in the 1980s

At the start of the 1980s there was a general feeling that poverty and social need had been eradicated in Norway. It was not long before sociologists discovered this to be a myth. A study from 1985 showed that around 5% of the population – roughly 200,000 people – could be regarded as the new poor. They included most elderly people, lone parents, those on disability allowance and the young unemployed. These people did not have to cope with hunger, cold, undernourishment and infectious disease, like poor people before them. Instead they struggled to raise the money for goods that the great majority took for granted.

The numbers of people on disability allowance rose greatly in the 1980s. One reason was that older people found it difficult to adjust to new ways of working. In 1987, a third of all Norwegians who reached pensionable age (67), were already in receipt of disability allowance, and during the Eighties the expenditure on social insurance rose from one eighth to one fifth of GNP.

The number of social security recipients almost trebled from 1980 to 1990. The big increase in unemployment and housing costs must carry a large proportion of the blame for the rise. During the 1980s an industrial worker had to pay out roughly five years' wages for a new house. In the 1950s he would have managed with just one year's money. With costs like these, there is little wonder that many jobless people could not make ends meet on unemployment benefit.

In the 1980s there was a lot of unease about the rapid rise of violent and drugs-related crime. The increase in suicide was hardly a healthy sign, either. But although social problems still existed, the average Norwegian's life was undoubtedly characterised by greater material prosperity and security than ever before. According to the UN's quality of life indices, Norway ranked very high.

Supporters and opponents of the EU prior to the referendum in 1994.

Norway's second no to Europe

In 1990 the question of Norway's relationship to the EC was again on the agenda. Together with the other EFTA countries, Norway began discussions with the EC on a new European Economic Area (EEA) agreement. Yet again, European politics caused collaborative trouble between the non-socialist parties. Disagreements over the economic working agreement led to the resignation of the Syse government, and in the autumn of 1991 Gro Harlem Brundtland formed a minority government for the third time.

In 1992 the negotiations with the EC were concluded. The EEA agreement paved the way for the free movement of goods, services, labour and capital between EFTA and EC countries. A common set of regulations was to ensure a level playing field for industry in all member countries. The agreement did not make Norway a member of the EC's supranational bodies. Nor was it a part of the common policy areas for agriculture, foreign or defence policy, but a majority of the *Storting* voted to make Norway an associate member of the Western European Union which was the EC's defence policy arm within NATO.

While the EEA negotiations were in progress, Sweden and Finland applied for membership of the EC which in 1993 had changed its name to the European Union (EU) after the Maastricht Treaty came into force. The treaty contained plans for an economic, monetary and foreign policy union in Europe. The Labour government decided to follow the example of its neighbours, and by the spring of 1994 the membership agreement between Norway and the EU was ready. An intense debate over Europe began, and it continued until the membership issue had been decided in a referendum in the autumn of the same year.

Essentially the debate revolved around the same arguments and contained the same factions as in 1972, but now it took place against a totally different European backdrop. At the time of the voting in the autumn of 1994, a majority of Austrians, Finns and Swedes had already said yes to membership. But these results made little difference to people's attitudes, and once again a small majority said no to European collaboration as set out in the Treaty of Rome.

Party politics and the economy at the turn of the millennium

In the last decades before the turn of the millenium salmon farming became an important industry in many coastal districts.

The Labour Party remained in power after the referendum and put all its energies into making the best of the EEA agreement. In the economic sphere, large parts of industry were rapidly drawn into the competition of the internal market. Simultaneously, new links were forged between Norway and the EU on provision of employment, conservation, culture, education and research. Furthermore the government started negotiations on the adoption of the so called Schengen Agreement, by which the border controls between Norway and the EU were abolished and police co-ordination increased. To a chorus of angry protests from anti-EU *Storting* members the Brundtland government hammered out an agreement on this, but it was put on hold when the EU countries decided to make the Schengen Agreement part of the supranational Treaty of Amsterdam.

The most serious conflict to arise between Norway and the EU concerned the trade in farmed salmon: Irish and Scottish fish farm-

ers accused Norwegian producers of dumping salmon on the European market and got the Commission in Brussels to bring in restrictions.

By the turn of the millennium the *Storting* had passed over 4,000 EU directives without using their veto rights from the EEA agreement. One of the most contentious was the "cosmetic foodstuffs directive", which permitted food additives that had previously been prohibited in Norway. A veterinary agreement was also signed which abolished the border controls on the trade in farm animals and animal products. Nor was there any hint of retaliation even when the EU passed a new gas directive that damaged Norway's interests. When the Union decided to establish a multinational crisis management force in 2000, Norway was prepared to put 3,500 soldiers at its disposal for such operations.

After Norway's experience of record levels of unemployment in the early 1990s, the period up to the turn of the millennium was characterised by an economic upturn. The development of oil and gas resources still required large investments, and the state began two expensive new building projects: a national hospital and a national airport. The Labour government also got a *Storting* mandate for extending basic schooling from nine to ten years. The large amount of activity in the economy needed more labour, and unemployment fell steadily. The Brundtland government got agreement from the main players in industry for a moderate wages policy, and this helped keep price rises low and interest rates falling. Meanwhile the receipts from oil and gas production increased so much that the state was able to set aside billions of kroner in an offshore fund which would help to lessen the pressures in the economy. There was broad political consensus that the oil fund should be a reserve to dip into in times of recession and for the benefit of future generations. By the end of 2002 the oil fund had topped 609 billion kroner.

In the autumn of 1996 Gro Harlem Brundtland was replaced by her party colleague Thorbjørn Jagland as prime minister. He had to conduct a wearying compromise policy in the *Storting*. Prior to the election the following year, Jagland demanded at least the same support from the voters as they had given in the previous election in 1993 (36.9%) if he was to continue, but the Labour Party failed to achieve that percentage. The election's winners were the Christian People's Party and the Progress Party, who each got the highest number of seats in parliament in their parties' history.

The election result paved the way for a centrist government with the Christian People's Party's Kjell Magne Bondevik as prime minister. This new minority government also included the Liberal and the Centre parties. Conditions did not allow a broader non-socialist coalition, principally because the differences between the Conservatives and the Centre Party had become insurmountable during and after the EU debate.

In 1998 the Christian People's Party succeeded in enacting one of its flagship policies: cash support for parents of young children without a playschool place. The same year the Bondevik government chose to bow to a *Storting* majority that wanted Norway to join the Schengen Agreement, but in 2000 the government refused to give way to a demand from the Conservatives and the Labour Party to build gas power stations, because it believed they caused too much pollution. This led to the one-party Labour government of Jens Stoltenberg, who retained power until the elections of 2001, when Kjell Magne Bondevik returned as prime minister, heading a coalition made up of the Christian People's Party, the Liberals and the Conservatives.

Norway, Europe and the world in the transition to a new millennium

The relaxation of tension in the north at the end of the Cold War meant that Norway occupied a more marginal place within the NATO alliance in the 1990s. At the same time, the disintegration of Yugoslavia meant that the alliance became more concerned with the military challenges in south-east Europe. Under these conditions it was important to strengthen ties with the USA. The Norwegian authorities consequently attached great importance to being allowed to keep the American contingency dumps in central Norway. Promises of continued American support were regarded as vital while the situation in Russia still had not stabilised.

In the new strategic picture Russia had lost important naval bases in the Baltic and had therefore become even more dependent on the Northern Fleet's bases on the Kola Peninsula. It was also becoming ever more apparent that these northern regions had a significant economic potential. Vast oil and gas fields were waiting to be developed both on shore and on the seabed in northern Russia. In addition, there was the possibility of a considerable Arctic boom if Russia opened the North-west Passage to shipping between Europe and Asia.

Co-operation with the new Russia in the 1990s had both its advances and its reverses. The so-called Barents Sea Co-operation, with a secretariat in Kirkenes, came into being in January 1993, with Norway, Sweden, Finland, Russia and the EU as participants. This regional initiative worked best in the cultural sphere but was viewed as less successful than the Baltic Sea Co-operation, which had been established at about the same time. Getting results in the areas of communications' development, economic life and environmental initiatives was a difficult process. Lack of Russian capital, mafia operations and an absence of legislation that could protect foreign investment, were the main roots of this lack of success. Another buffer to co-operation was the fact that Norway and Russia were unable to reach final agreement about the demarcation line in the Barents Sea.

During the 1990s the aims of development aid were changed. Greater emphasis was now placed on whether the recipient nations had the ability to work for human rights, democratic governmental reforms and policies of social distribution. Bad experiences with a number of aid projects and the fear that help would lead to aid-dependency and thus stand in the way of development, contributed

to lowering the priority of the long-term aid projects. Traditional Third World aid was now seen in the same context as other elements in a new humanitarian foreign policy: Norway was to stand out in the world community with crisis aid campaigns, participation in peace keeping military operations and peace mediation.

Norwegian mediators took part in the peace processes in Sri Lanka, El Salvador, Sudan, Nicaragua and the former Yugoslavia. International attention focused mainly on the Norwegian contribution to the peace process in the Middle East which led to what became known as the Oslo Accord between Israel and the PLO in 1993.

With the centenary of the dissolution of the union with Sweden imminent, Norway was facing an important crossroads. Should the country continue its lonely sojourn as an open-handed peace mediator, like some resource-rich, specially-exempt Nordic Switzerland, outside the European process of integration? This would mean that her long heritage of neutrality and missionary work would have prevailed and that Norway would have to toil onward in the turbulent waters between the EU and the USA. Or would the country get caught up in the undertow of EU enlargement in Eastern Europe and finally say yes to membership of the European Union? Such a development would show that the free trade and alliance tradition had got the upper hand and that dogged Norwegian isolationism had been dealt a fatal blow.

The awarding of the Nobel Peace Prize is one of the few events that really puts Norway on the international map. By presenting the prize to Yasir Arafat, Menachem Begin and Shimon Peres in 1994, the Norwegian Nobel Committee were trying to stimulate the peace process in the Middle East, the so-called Oslo Process.

It was a great day in the
Norwegian royal family's
history when Crown
Prince Haakon married
Mette-Marit Tjessem
Høiby in August 2001.
After the wedding the
couple received the ova-
tion of the crowd from the
palace balcony together
with the King and Queen.
The Crown Princess is
carrying her son Marius.

Name index

Arafat, Yasir 177
Albrecht of Mecklenburg 45, 46
Amundsen, Roald 108, 114
Begin, Menachem 177
Bell, Alexander Graham 86
Bjørnson, Bjørnstjerne 91, 93, 97
Bondevik, Kjell Magne 175
Borten, Per 147, 151
Bratteli, Trygve 151, 152
Brun, Johan Nordahl 64
Brundtland, Gro Harlem 159, 167, 171, 172, 174, 175
Carl 12. 62
Carl 13. 68, 71, 75
Carl Johan 68, 71, 72, 75, 77, 78, 79, 80
Chamberlain, Neville 122
Christian 2. 46, 47
Christian 3. 46, 49
Christian 4. 49, 51, 52, 53, 54, 60
Christian Frederik 71, 72, 73, 74, 75, 77
Christie, Wilhelm F. K. 67
Churchill, Winston 118, 122
Elsworth, Lincoln 114
Eirik the Red 25, 26
Leiv Eirikson 25, 27
Eric of Pomerania 46
Erik of Södermanland 42
Eriksen, Stein 138
Erling Skakke 38, 39
Falsen, Christian Magnus 67, 72
Frederik 3. 52, 54, 55, 56
Frederik 4. 61, 62
Frederik 6. 68, 69, 71, 72
Garborg, Arne 90
Gaulle, Charles de 146
Gerhardsen, Einar 133, 137, 140
Grieg, Edvard 91
Gustav 4. Adolf 68
Gyldenløve, Ulrik Frederik 58
Hagen, Carl I. 167
Hamsun, Knut 103
Harald 5. 178

Harald Gille 38
Harald Hardrada 36
Harald Fairhair 25, 27
Hauge, Frederic 167
Hauge, Hans Nielsen 63, 64, 71
Heyerdahl, Thor 168
Haakon 7. 96, 97, 123
Haakon, Crown Prince 178
Håkon 5. Magnusson 42, 45
Håkon the Good 28
Håkon Håkonsson 40, 42
Hitler, Adolf 117, 118, 119, 121, 123, 126
Ibsen, Henrik 85, 92, 93
Ingebjørg 42
Jaabæk, Søren 89, 90
Jagland, Thorbjørn 175
Jarlsberg, Herman Wedel 67, 71, 74
Jeltsin, Boris 174
Keynes, John Maynard 113
Kielland, Alexander 92
Knut the Great 31, 33
Lofthus, Christian Jensen 63, 71
Luther, Martin 46
Lyng, John 147
Magnus Eriksson 45
Magnus Erlingsson 38, 40
Magnus Lagabøte 41
Magnus Sigurdsson 37
Margrete 45, 46
Maud 97
Mette-Marit, Crown Princess 178
Montesquieu, Charles de Secondant 74
Michelsen, Christian 96, 97, 99, 108
Munch, Edvard 92
Napoleon Bonaparte 67, 68
Næss, Arne 150
Nansen, Fridtjof 95, 108, 112, 116
Nobile, Umberto 114
Nygaardsvold, Johan 122, 128
Olav 4. 46
Olav Engelbrektsson 46
Olav Haraldsson 31
Olav, Crown Prince 96, 97, 123, 129
Olav Tryggvason 29